The Gift of Being

A Theology of Creation

Zachary Hayes, O.F.M.

A Michael Glazier Book
THE LITURGICAL PRESS
Collegeville, Minnesota
www.litpress.org

NEW THEOLOGY STUDIES
General Editor: Peter C. Phan

*

Editorial Consultants:
Monika Hellwig
Robert Imbelli
Robert Schreiter

*

Volume 10: The Gift of Being: A Theology of Creation

A Michael Glazier Book published by Liturgical Press.

Cover design by David Manahan, O.S.B.

ISBN 13: 978-0-8146-5941-0
ISBN 10: 0-8146-5941-1

7   8

Library of Congress Cataloging-in-Publication Data

Hayes, Zachary.
  Gift of being : a theology of creation / Zachary Hayes.
    p.   cm. — (New theology studies ; v. 10)
  "A Michael Glazier book."
  Includes bibliographical references and index.
  ISBN 0-8146-5941-1 (alk. paper)
    1. Creation. 2. Creation—Biblical teaching. 3. Nature—Religious aspects—Christianity. 4. Human ecology—Religious aspects—Christianity. I. Title. II. Series.

BT695 .H32   2000
231.7'65—dc21

                                                             00-030151

Contents

Editor's Preface

This series entitled *New Theology Studies* is an attempt to answer the need felt by professors and students alike for scholarly yet readable books dealing with certain Catholic beliefs traditionally associated with dogmatic theology. The volumes in the series treat of fundamental theology (revelation, the nature and method of theology, the credibility of the Christian faith), trinitarian theology, christology, ecclesiology, anthropology, and eschatology.

There has been, of course, no lack of books, published singly or in series, both in this continent and elsewhere, which are concerned with these central truths of Christianity. Nevertheless, there is room, we believe, for yet another series of texts on systematic theology, not because these offer entirely novel insights into the aforementioned teachings, but because it is incumbent upon Christians of every age to reflect upon their faith in light of their cultural and religious experiences and to articulate their understanding in terms accessible to their contemporaries.

Theology is traditionally described as faith in search of understanding, *fides quaerens intellectum*. The faith to which the contributors to this series are committed is the Christian faith as lived and taught by the (Roman) catholic church. It is, however, a faith that is ecumenically sensitive, open to ways of living and thinking practiced by other Christian communities and other religions. The understanding which the series seeks to foster goes beyond an accumulation of information, however interesting, on the Christian past to retrieve and renew, by means of the analogical imagination, the Christian tradition embodied in its various classics. In this way, it is hoped, one can understand afresh both the meaning and the truth of the Christian beliefs and their multiple interconnections. Lastly, the contributors are convinced that theology is a never-ending quest for insights into faith, a *cogitatio fidei.* Its ultimate purpose is not to provide definite and definitive answers to every conceivable problem posed by faith, but to gain an understanding, which will always be imperfect and fragmentary, of its subject, God the incomprehensible Mystery. Thus, theology remains an essentially unfinished business to be taken up over and again in light of and in confrontation with the challenges found in every age. And our age is no exception, when, to cite only two examples, massive poverty and injustice structured into the present economic order, and the unprecedented meeting of religious faiths in new contexts of dialogue, have impelled theologians to reconceptualize the Christian faith in radical terms.

Contrary to some recent series of textbooks, *New Theology Studies* does not intend to advocate and advance a uniform or even unified viewpoint. Contributors are left free to present their own understanding and approach to the subject matter assigned to them. They are only requested to treat their themes in an integrating manner by situating them in the context of Tradition (highlighting their biblical, patristic, medieval, and modern developments), by expounding their theological meaning and function in light of current pronouncements of the Magisterium, by exploring their implications for Christian living, and by indicating possible different contemporary conceptualizations of these doctrines. The goal is to achieve some measure of comprehensiveness and balance by taking into account all the important issues of the subject matter under discussion and at the same time exhibit some thematic unity by means of a consistent method and a unifying perspective.

The volumes are intended primarily as resource books, "launching and landing bases," for upper-division theology courses in Catholic colleges and seminaries, but it is hoped that they will be useful also to people—priests, permanent deacons, religious, and educated laity, inside and outside of the Roman Catholic communion—interested in understanding the Christian faith in contemporary cultural and ecclesial contexts. We hope that these volumes will make a contribution, however modest, to the intellectual and spiritual life of the Christian Church as it prepares to enter its third millennium.

Peter C. Phan
The Catholic University of America

Introduction

The primary concern in this book is to reflect on what is seen as the traditional task of creation-theology in Christian theological history. We will attempt to do this by bringing major concerns of the tradition into some relationship with issues raised by the contemporary sciences, particularly the theory of biological evolution and the new vision of physical cosmology which has become so widely known not only to professional scientists but to the public at large.

When we speak of the traditional task of creation-theology, we have in mind the way in which creation-theology was typically the place in which theology attempted to lay out a convincing road-map of reality that could help believers do a number of important things. If the road-map worked, it would help people to come to a stronger sense of their own identity as they came to an awareness of the nature of the world in which they found themselves. This would enable them, in turn, to gain a deeper insight into how they ought to relate to that sort of world if they wished to find meaning in their lives.

In the past this has meant a number of important things. First, it has required the willingness to distinguish between the medium and message in approaching the Scriptures. We have in mind a process known already to the Patristic authors and followed by the Scholastic authors of the medieval period. These writers commonly were convinced that, while the Bible did have a literal, historical meaning, the true religious meaning of the text would be found only through some form of spiritual interpretation. This commonly involved a form of allegorical and moral interpretation. Allegorization, however, did not begin with the Fathers. It was practiced already by the biblical authors themselves in both the Hebrew Scriptures and in the

Christian Scriptures. In the latter, this was a common technique through which the history depicted in the Hebrew Scriptures could be brought into a Christian context and be appropriated in relation to a new experience. Thus, while it was hardly contestable to Patristic or Scholastic commentators that the Bible had a literal meaning, the bulk of their writings gives little evidence of the sort of radical fundamentalism we have come to see in the modern and contemporary era of Christian history. For us, with respect to this sacred text, this will require the willingness to distinguish between the religious message communicated through the revelatory process that gave rise to the Bible on the one hand, and the physical vision of the cosmos which provides the framework within which the religious meaning is projected.

Second, in the past this theological task required a willingness to take with appropriate seriousness the best available natural understanding of the world, both in terms of physics and in terms of metaphysics. This means that in our theological tradition, theology was not merely a question of repeating what seemed to be the teachings of the Bible. It included also the attempt to situate that teaching in a world-view unknown to the biblical authors. From early in Christian history, theology was understood to be "faith in search of understanding." And the search for understanding involved the use of the human mind in the attempt to discern the deeper levels of meaning.

As we will see, the willingness to operate in terms of these two suppositions made it possible for Christians in different periods to create powerful, convincing world-views which embraced the message of the Bible, but spoke of it in terms of philosophical and physical insights that were unknown to the biblical authors. Our primary concern is to explore some of the possibilities of doing a similar thing today for our time and place.

A final word about the scientific issues we will be concerned with is in place. We do not intend to make this a sort of scientific handbook. But we are convinced that there are a number of basic characteristics involved in the contemporary physical understanding of the created cosmos that can be singled out without committing ourselves to a particular physical theory or cosmological model. We have in mind the pervasive sense, regardless as to how it is explained, that the cosmos in which we find ourselves is far more immense in space and time than we have ever envisioned in the past, and that it is not yet complete. It is still in the process of becoming.

We are quite convinced also that it is a highly unified chemical system which seems to involve relations among its components at every level we have been able to investigate to this point. This seems to hold true as far down as we have been able to go into quark research, and as far outward as we have been able to go with our highly developed telescopes. It is out of this immensely fascinating cosmic process that, in this particular planet of this particular galaxy, life has emerged in many forms, and specifically in the form of intelligent, conscious life. Until now, we are the only instance of this in the entire cosmos of which we have clear knowledge. In this sense, then, we can say that humanity is the cosmic process as it has become living, intelligent, and conscious of itself in this sector of the cosmos. Who are we, then? We who find ourselves in this fascinating, puzzling cosmos. Are we perhaps the *Lonely Hearts of the Cosmos?*[1] How are we to understand ourselves and our world as it is described to us through contemporary science? And what sense of meaning can our biblical and theological tradition offer us as we contemplate this reality?

These are the kinds of questions that have suggested the structure and the discussion in the following chapters. Our intent is to address a public that is literate though not professional in the sciences, and to provide at least the starting point for a theological understanding of the issues that surface for anyone who takes our scientific culture seriously.

Our presentation will not treat all the traditional topics found in the handbook treatment of creation-theology. Rather, we shall attempt to open a number of the crucial areas which would be basic to any fuller development in relation to the issues raised for theology by the world of the sciences. We will begin by discussing the relation between faith and reason, and hence between theology and science, from an historical perspective, moving to the most current statements of modern popes. This will be of particular interest for those who stand within the Roman Catholic tradition since other streams of Christian tradition suggest quite different approaches. This will be followed by a summary statement of the possible retrieval of the biblical religious insights that can be legitimately distinguished from the physical world-view that seems to stand behind much of the biblical material, at least in the view of many critical biblical scholars.

The above will clear the ground for a discussion of the traditional concept of creation from nothing in the form of a conversation with contemporary physics. This will be followed by a discussion not of some generic idea of God, but specifically of the Christian idea of God as the primal mystery of creative love from whom all of creation flows. With these foundational ideas in place, we will then look at the questions about humanity in such an understanding; the origin of humanity, and the failure of humanity throughout its history. This will be followed by a discussion of what might best be called the tradition of cosmic christology. Our concern will be to highlight the key insights of such a tradition and to ask about

[1] Cfr. Dennis Overbye, *Lonely Hearts of the Cosmos: The Story of the Scientific Quest for the Secret of the Universe* (New York: HarperCollins, 1991).

how they might be reflected on in our contemporary context. Finally, the theological issue of the final outcome of God's creation and its history will be discussed against the background of the current scientific projections of a future for the cosmos.

With that we will have dealt with the crucial building-blocks for what could eventually be developed into a fuller theology of creation. It is our hope that the issues we discuss will indicate the possibilities of relating the deep concerns of tradition with the present insights of the sciences in a way that is helpful for the increasingly educated Christian consciousness of the modern world.

1

Science, the Bible, and Christianity

In the context of contemporary Western culture, many are convinced that there is, of necessity, some deep and abiding conflict between the biblical vision of reality and the work of the sciences. Others are convinced that even though there are, in fact, obvious conflicts between particular ways of reading the Bible and particular claims of science, this does not mean that there is an inevitable conflict in principle. Such conflicts may, in fact, reveal a poor understanding of the Bible, and/or a misunderstanding of the nature of scientific claims. However one assesses the situation, anyone whose understanding is grounded in a deeper knowledge of the Christian tradition does not need to be forced to choose between the Bible and science.

The relation between religious faith and the sciences is a distinctively modern way of experiencing an issue which has long been present in Christian history. In the most basic sense, it is the question of the relation between reason and faith; between natural knowledge and knowledge allegedly based on some form of special divine revelation. In certain periods of history, the claims of natural knowledge that dominated the stage were those of philosophy though other forms of natural knowledge were not excluded. At the present time, when we speak of natural knowledge, there is a great emphasis on the sort of knowledge mediated through the positive sciences, though other forms of knowledge are not automatically excluded. In Christian history the theology of creation has been the place where elements of the biblical tradition have interacted with various forms of natural knowledge, including a number of different philosophies as well as with physical cosmology. The early periods of this history are not the private reserve of the Roman Catholic tradition. But Roman Catholic theology has appropriated the insights of the earlier historical moments in its own distinctive way.

I) *Early and Medieval Christian History*

In the early centuries of Christian history, a clear instance of the interaction between reason and faith may be found in the work of St. Augustine (354–430 C.E.). In his case, the natural knowledge involved was mainly that of philosophy; and the philosophy involved was that of neo-Platonism with its doctrine of emanationism, the divine Ideas, and exemplarity. In such a philosophical context Augustine was able to see the created cosmos as a vast song of God, or as a book in which the intelligence and love of God has expressed itself. All who are able to hear the song that the cosmos sings, or to read this cosmic book will discover important insights into the meaning of the divine and into the direction and purpose of human life.

There is, however, another book; namely the book of the Scriptures. During the course of his life, Augustine commented on the opening chapters of the book of Genesis not only once, but several times. And his understanding shifts from one time to the next. He may be seen as a good example of a person who was willing to take up significant questions over and over, and who came to the end of his career without having a final answer to the problems with which he had struggled for so long. Obviously, along the way he has written opinions which many will find problematic when viewed from a modern perspective. But perhaps what is most significant is not a particular statement he has made, but the dynamism of the process which carried him throughout his career.

In a work entitled *The Literal Meaning of Genesis,* Augustine argued that a proper understanding of this text should not contradict what one rightfully holds about the heavens and the earth from reason and from experience.[1] And he warns against interpretations of Scripture that any well-instructed non-believer would recognize as nonsense. It is clear that Augustine himself believed that God created all things in one act in the beginning. But it is likewise clear that, in his view, not all things existed in their individual, finished forms from the start. Augustine used the idea of seminal reasons to explain in what sense all things were given in seed-form in the beginning, and yet appeared in their particularity only as time passed on. Every form of life was given in the mind of God from the beginning. But they were actualized in time as material realities realized their God-given potentialities. In no sense was this a theory of evolution as we know

---

[1] *The Literal Meaning of Genesis*, tr. J. H. Taylor, vol. 41–42 in: *Ancient Christian Writers* (New York: Newman Press, 1982).

it today. It was a limited way in which he could envision some form of development within creation in terms of the categories of his time.

The Bible, argues Augustine, should not be seen as a scientific book. It is, rather, a book of truth concerning human salvation. As a number of modern authors have phrased it, Augustine suggests that the Bible tells us how to get to heaven; but it does not tell us how the heavens go. Since both the book of the cosmos and the book of the Scriptures come from the same primal truth, in principle there ought to be no contradiction between them. The genius of Augustine was able to create a powerful religious cosmology in the light of which Christians could define the meaning of their lives for many centuries of Christian history. As people of faith, they did not have to fear looking out at the physical cosmos to discover what it could tell them concerning the mystery of the divine.

In the medieval period, theologians such as St. Bonaventure, following the lead of Augustine, could see the created cosmos as the primal revelation of God and did not hesitate to compare it to a book. The content of the book of the cosmos is the divine Ideas or archetypes. The task of human beings is to learn how to read this book and thus to discover something about the mystery of the divine Creator-Artisan as they learn to understand the world more deeply.

St. Thomas Aquinas could formulate what would represent a common Scholastic position; namely, that in principle, there cannot be a contradiction between natural revelation as given in the created order and supernatural revelation as given in the biblical history. Since both are grounded in the same God whose truth is abiding, these two modalities of divine revelation cannot be in conflict. It may happen, however, that something more may be communicated in the biblical revelation than what is communicated in the natural revelation alone. Thus, while the two levels of revelation will not conflict with each other, it is not only possible but it is a fact that the biblical revelation goes beyond what may be known from the cosmic revelation. This is particularly the case with regard to those matters involved in the Christian understanding of salvation and the way in which the possibility of salvation has been opened to humanity.

The theology of Aquinas himself particularly highlights the influence of Aristotle on Western Christian thought even while it maintains significant elements of the neo-Platonic tradition. The discovery of the entire corpus of the philosopher's writings was first the concern of medieval Arab scholars in Spain. From there the works of Aristotle entered the world of Christian scholarship in the major countries on the European continent as well as in England. To the scholars of that time, Aristotle appeared to be simply the best that the human mind had accomplished up till then. But he was significantly different from Plato, and he seemed to stand for a number of philosophical positions that were in conflict with the Bible. What was one to do in the face of such a challenge? Simply put, the familiar theology of some seven or eight centuries was now being challenged by a philosophical world-view that had been unknown in Europe until then, and that had convincing power for many intellectuals of that time. Does one ignore it because it seems to conflict with basic issues of theology and faith? Or does one somehow engage it in a critical and creative way?

Simply stated, there was not one uniform reaction to this problem. Some resisted Aristotle vigorously. Others engaged his thought with different degrees of critical sensitivity. But in the long run, this engagement left a style of theological cosmology which was to have wide-reaching impact on Western Christian thought, and in a particular way, on Catholic thought.

This engagement brought together elements of the biblical tradition with the metaphysics and the physics of Aristotle. To understand what was attempted here, it is important to keep in mind the basic conviction which medieval authors could trace back to Augustine, and from which they worked: the God who creates and is therefore revealed in the cosmos is the same God who is revealed in the historical revelation that led to the writing of the Bible. If this is the case, and if we think of God as the primal truth, this must mean that there should be no contradiction between these two forms of revelation: the cosmic and the historical.

In the medieval context, this was formulated in terms of the relation between knowledge (or reason) and faith (related to religious revelation). The traditional program of "faith in search of understanding" could now be carried out with a new understanding of the range of reason, including the logic, physics, metaphysics, and ethics of Aristotle. The work of the Scholastics, then, involved the creation of a road-map of reality considerably different from that commonly associated with the Bible, particularly with the opening chapters of the book of Genesis.

When we speak of metaphysics, we are referring to a philosophical attempt to describe the larger structures of reality. In the most basic sense, metaphysics is concerned with the mystery of being. What does it mean to be? As it relates to the issue of creation, metaphysics helps theology to express the mystery of the absolute origin of reality in the creative love of God. This is one of the most basic functions of metaphysics within the theology of creation. At another level, metaphysics will attempt to show the relation between the constant change in the world of our empirical experience and the human concern for finding something with greater permanence. The Aristotelian metaphysics sees that which is permanent as more basic than change. It sees a world of unchanging natures which, at the level of natures, has always been the same. What comes and goes are the individual, historical beings that embody a nature to a limited extent. A human being, for example, is born as a potential knower. By reason of its nature, says Aristotle, it is a rational animal. That has always been the nature of human beings, and always will be. Change takes place within the framework of the movement from the state of potential knower to that of an actual knower. It is in the latter state that the potential of human nature is realized. Thus, for Aristotle, there is change and development. But the limits of change are defined by the unchanging nature of things. Since nature defines species, it follows that development cannot be from one species to another species. It can take place only within the limits of the species, as individuals move from potency to act.

So there was a metaphysics developed first by Greek philosophers, and later employed by Christian theologians to develop their theological insights. This metaphysics was probably unknown to the authors of the Bible. Beyond the issue of metaphysics, there was a physics. Here we need to recall the typical description of the physical cosmology in the background of much of the Hebrew Scriptures, particularly of the opening chapters of Genesis. The earth itself appeared to be a flat shelf. The shelf of the earth was supported by pillars that held the earth above the abyss. The dome of the firmament soared above with the heavenly bodies and the flood gates, etc. By the time we get to the thirteenth century, this physical cosmology has been replaced by that of Aristotle (384/3–322/1 B.C.E.) and Ptolemy (ca. 87–170 C.E.). This new physical view could be expressed clearly by Bonaventure in the following way:

> The entire fabric of the physical world consists in the heavenly and the elemental natures. Heavenly nature comprises three main heavens: the empyrean heaven, the crystalline heaven, and the firmament. Beneath the firmament, which is the heaven of stars, are the seven spheres of the planets: Saturn, Jupiter, Mars, and Sun, Venus, Mercury, and the Moon. Elemental nature is divided into four spheres: Fire, Air, Water, and Earth.[2]

This is not the physical world-view of the Bible. It is unmistakably the physical world-view as articulated by Aristotle and Ptolemy. And this physical world-view is now brought into context of theology.

Neither the *Summa contra Gentiles* nor the final *Summa* of Aquinas speak in such detail of this physical cosmology. But in the *Summa*, Aquinas speaks in a way that reflects this physics. He speaks of four things that are created at once and together. These are: the empyrean heavens, bodily matter (i.e., the earth), time, and the angelic nature.[3]

---

[2] *Breviloquium* 2, 3 (V, 220–21). References to works of Bonaventure will be to the Quaracchi edition. Volume number is the Roman number in parentheses, followed by page number.
[3] *Sth.* I, q. 46, a.3.

If we look closer at the work of the thirteenth century, we find some truly unexpected things. We find theologians debating about the possible eternity of the world. We discover theologians speculating about the possibility of a plurality of worlds. We find a remarkable sense of the radical contingence of this particular, actual world, together with a conviction of its basic intelligibility. What is impressive is not so much the correctness or incorrectness of their answers, but the range of questions generated by the attempt of theology to engage what seemed to them to be some of the best insights of human reason. And what came out of this was a well-integrated vision of reality that embraced physics and metaphysics and the faith-vision of Christianity. The world about which theology reflected was the same physical world about which Aristotle and Ptolemy had attempted to speak. And theology could help orient human life in that sort of world. If the scientific viewpoint was an accurate account of the world, there should not be a conflict with the vision of faith. If there seems to be, one must search for an understanding that can resolve the difference.

Thus, when we look at the medieval theological construct, we find a well-knit interrelation of faith, metaphysics, and physics. The metaphysics and physics of Aristotle was seen as simply the best the human mind had been able to come up with in describing the cosmos. This described for people of that time and place a cosmos within which one could situate humanity and come to some sense of the human relationship to the whole. This was the result of the medieval encounter between faith and physical cosmology. The power of this vision can be seen in the *Divine Comedy* of Dante. There, in the form of great poetic literature, the reader is taken on a tour of this cosmos from level to level, until in the *Paradiso* one is drawn into the mystical contemplation of the creative, divine Light as one is drawn from one sphere to another, coming ever closer to that Pure Light that dwells beyond the realm of fire—the Empyrean.

We might say, in the words of Peter Berger, that they created a sacred canopy, a total picture of the world in which the believer lives.[4] This canopy does at the intellectual level of medieval Europe what religious myths had done at an earlier level of religious history. It creates a safe-zone in what otherwise might seem to be a puzzling, chaotic, threatening world. Within that safe-zone, people can come to live with a firm sense of identity and purpose. In what follows, we will see a classic case of what happens when something threatens someone's safe-zone.

One can come out of the encounter with medieval theology with the following convictions. (1) For medieval theologians there is no Christian the-

---

[4] P. Berger, *The Sacred Canopy: Elements of a Sociological Theory of Religion* (Garden City: Doubleday, 1969).

ology without at least an implicit physical cosmology. (2) The world of physics helps to provide some insight into what the world of creation actually looks like and how it operates and undergoes change. These issues will be discussed further in later chapters.

II) *The Work of Copernicus (1473–1543) and Galileo (1564–1642)*

The significance of these two names in the history of Western thought may be seen in the fact that the term *Copernican revolution* has become a common way of describing any major shift in thought; and the name *Galileo* almost automatically triggers the sense of inevitable conflict between Christian faith and science. In no way can we deal with this issue in detail. But we would like to show at least that there is no need to see these two names as symptomatic of an inevitable state of warfare between religion and scientific investigation.

There were issues involved in the very understanding of science that called into question the fundamental validity of the Aristotelian tradition of natural philosophy. The later medieval period had seen the work of a number of scholars who began the process of questioning the validity of the Aristotelian-Ptolemaic world view. A more gradual historical process has been traced than the usual stereotypical vision of some sort of abrupt break coming with Copernicus and Galileo.[5]

There was, as well, a situation of religious unrest unleashed by the Protestant Reformation. Martin Luther died just three years after the death of Copernicus, in 1546. Questions concerning the proper interpretation of the Scriptures were unavoidable at the time. How does one deal with the tradition of the Church Fathers? And in the context of the Council of Trent and its concern with Reformation theology, how does one deal with the teaching authority of the Church in respect to the proper interpretation of Scripture.

Given all this in the historical background, it is important to recognize also: (1) How tightly the Ptolemaic physical cosmology was integrated into the theology and culture of medieval Europe; and (2) the feeling of threat and danger that ensues whenever an important frame-work of meaning is threatened, regardless of where the threat comes from. So when the work of Copernicus and Galileo made a strong case for the change from a geocentric vision to a heliocentric vision, this was not just a simple, theoretical idea of some adventuresome investigators. It was not simply a

---

[5] The argument for some form of gradualism has been made by P. Duhem, *Medieval Cosmology: Theories of Infinity, Place, Time, Void, and the Plurality of Worlds*, ed. and tr. by R. Ariew (Chicago: University of Chicago Press, 1985) and by S. Jaki, *Science and Creation: From Eternal Cycles to an Oscillating Universe* (Edinburgh: Scottish Academy Press, 1986).

question of rearranging the furniture on the deck of a ship. It was, in fact, a vision that threatened the loss of the entire ship. It is a new physical cosmology projected into a culturally and religiously complex situation that creates the problem. The poem of John Donne expresses this with great power.

> And new Philosophy calls all in doubt,
> The Element of fire is quite put out;
> The Sun is lost, and th'earth, and no man's wit
> Can well direct him, where to looke for it . . .
> 'Tis all in pieces, all cohearence gone;
> All just supply, and all Relation. . . .
> For the world's beauty is decayed, or gone,
> Beauty, that's color, and proportion.[6]

The point of this poem can be given in a single word: *anomie*. In terms of its etymology, this term comes from the Greek word *nomos* which means order, or law. The prefix *a* is the simple negation of the primary noun. Therefore the word means: without order, or without law. The *American Heritage Dictionary* gives the following definitions: (1) The collapse of the social structures governing a society; (2) the state of alienation experienced by an individual or a class in such a situation; (3) personal disorganization resulting in unsocial behavior.[7] We might think of this as analogous to an attempt to travel through an uncharted wilderness when one has no map, and there are no signs. What would that feel like?

This might help to make the reaction to the view of Copernicus and Galileo more understandable. The problem is not just an issue of stubborn ecclesiastics concerned with church-political problems, though such issues were certainly a part of the problem. From one perspective, the new view seemed to fly in the face of common-sense observations. Everyone in the Western world (which is what was involved at this time) sees the sun rise in the East, move to the South, and set in the West. We see the sun's arc increase as we move into the summer. We see it decrease as we move toward winter. Common sense tells us that the sun moves through the sky. Never, on the other hand, do we feel or see the earth moving. From another perspective, the idea that the earth moves did not seem to measure up to the then operative understanding of scientific knowledge. The issues involved in the heliocentric vision, at least then, did not seem to measure up as science.

The geocentric view had the distinct advantage of placing the planet on which human beings live in the very center of the cosmic order. This made

---

[6] *The Complete Poetry of John Donne*, ed. J. T. Shawcross. With introduction, notes and variants. The Anchor-Seventeenth Century series (New York, 1967) 277–78.
[7] 2nd ed., 112.

it fairly easy to move from a geocentric sense to an anthropocentric sense. Not only is the earth at the physical center, but humanity is at the center of the entire picture. If the earth is moved out of the center, what are we to think of humanity? Who are we? And what sort of world do we live in if we can no longer trust some of our most basic physical experiences?

The reaction of church authorities seems heavy-handed to us today. And it took a long time for the highest authorities to admit that theologians erred in claiming that the opening lines of Sacred Scripture described the physical, mechanical working of the universe, and that the church officials had erred in condemning Galileo. But on October 31, 1992, Pope John Paul II lifted the condemnation of Galileo and of his view.

However we might assess this entire case in retrospect, the affair signaled the beginning of a long-standing and unfortunate separation of theology and science with very important implications. Science would go on its own way, developing its own methodology and its instruments for closer observation. This is not to say that scientists were atheists by virtue of the fact that they were scientists. But their work, regardless of their personal motivations, seemed profoundly threatening to many. Theology would continue to express itself in terms of language and categories of what seemed to be an increasingly archaic physical cosmology. More and more the believer seemed to be torn between two worlds with little to mediate between them.

III) *From Galileo to Darwin*

Thus, roughly from the time of Galileo to that Charles Darwin (1809–1882), there was commonly a feeling of distrust among theologians concerning the direction taken by the sciences. For the most part, the dominant model operative in dealing with science and theology was one of suspicion. At this level, the issue was, to a great extent, the tension created by two large, conflicting models of physical cosmology. But in the nineteenth century things would become even more tense. Now it was not simply a question about the implications of a heliocentric cosmology. It was a question of the cosmic roots of the human species within the framework of a theory of biological evolution. At one level, the theory of evolution seemed to fly in the face of the Aristotelian view of species and natures which had been operative in Western Christian thought since the thirteenth century. No such thing as a trans-species development was metaphysically possible. Only change and growth within the limits of an unchanging species could be envisioned.

However one understands the view of Darwin, his theory, as well as other developmental theories, seem to imply quite a different understanding of species and the origin of species. When Aristotle defined the human person as a rational animal, the term *rational* was a way of stating something that made human beings essentially different from other animals known as *the brutes*. In simple medieval Latin, "bruta carent intellectu." The brute animals have no intellect. Human beings do. But now theories of evolution seemed to dethrone humanity and to bring with it the end of the metaphysics of the immutable and essentially different species. Evolutionary theories, moving from Darwin to the present, seem to blur the lines of distinction between brutes and humans. How can we maintain a genuine sense of human dignity when science points more and more to our chemical rootage in the cosmic process, and our specific rootage in the animal world?

Without going into detail, let us simply say that the views of evolutionary thought tended to solidify the popular mistrust of the sciences, and confirmed a sense of conflict between science and theology. If science seems to tear down the structures through which human beings can create a sense of identity and meaning, then perhaps science is the enemy. One does not consort with the enemy. One fights it.

IV) *The New Physics*

In the twentieth-century the loss of a physical center in the cosmos becomes even more dramatic. When one thinks of the implications of relativity-theory, quantum-physics, and Big Bang cosmology, it seems safe to say that there is no physical center in such a cosmos. Or, perhaps there are as many centers as there are observers searching for such a thing.

At the same time, Christian theology gradually has come to a fuller sense of the degree to which it is historically situated and limited. And theology has recovered a sense of the principle that stood behind the medieval synthesis: The God who creates and is thus revealed in the cosmos is the God who is revealed in biblical history. Since this is the case, in principle there ought to be no contradiction between cosmic revelation and the religious insights communicated through biblical history. The believer should be able to look out at the same world described by the sciences and see precisely that world as the world of God's creation.

In understanding this, it is important to keep in mind the caution which we have already seen as far back as Augustine: The message of the Bible is not about the physics of the universe, but about the truth of human salvation that becomes conscious for us in the history that creates the Bible. With this in mind, we turn to some of the more recent shifts in Roman Catholic thinking on the relation between science and theology, specifically in number of recent papal statements.

V) *Statements of Popes*

In 1950 Pope Pius XII issued the encyclical letter *Humani generis*. Among other things, this encyclical addressed the question of biological evolution. Thus, it was concerned with a specific issue, and not with the larger issue of scientific cosmology. The details of the papal discussion on evolution will be discussed in a later chapter. For now, we wish only to point out that the Pope saw no necessary conflict between science and religion. While it is clear that the encyclical hardly commends an ongoing interaction between theology and science, neither does it condemn the scientific theories with which it is concerned.

In 1951 the same Pope issued a statement in which he praised the work of the sciences generally, and the work of Hubble leading to the idea of an expanding cosmos. In all of this the Pope saw the sort of work that not only unveils the secrets of nature, but precisely in doing so, discloses the creative work of God. He judged that the theory of the expanding cosmos gave eloquent scientific testimony to something that was known already as true from the biblical revelation: namely, the temporal beginning of creation.[8]

Many theologians have been negative in their reaction to this statement, feeling that it reflected a dubious understanding of the nature of the sciences, as well as a problematic understanding of the biblical texts of Genesis. Thus, while at first reading, the statement of Pius XII might have seemed to be a significant step in seeking some positive relation between science and theology, it has been seen by many to suggest an unfortunate direction. Whatever relation one might seek between science and theology, it is not helpful to look to science for some sort of apologetic proof for religious faith, whatever form that proof might take. As John Casti writes: "A theology that attaches itself to one scientific family today will surely be an orphan tomorrow."[9] Hence from the early 1950s Catholics generally have shied away from such an apologetic approach.

Pope John Paul II has addressed the question of science and theology on a number of occasions. In 1982 he spoke to a gathering of scientists in Rome.[10] On this occasion, he placed science in the context of a social mission, emphasizing the moral character of the scientist in relation to the general good of humanity, and highlighting the role of science in the building of human culture. He appealed for collaboration between the disciplines of

[8] Pius XII, "Modern Science and the Existence of God," in: *The Catholic Mind* (March 1952) 182–92.

[9] *Paradigms Lost: Tackling the Unanswered Mysteries of Modern Science* (New York: Avon Books, 1989) 65.

[10] "Science and Progress," Discourse to participants at a convention sponsored by the National Academy of Sciences; September 21, 1982, *The Pope Speaks* 27 (Winter 1982) 365.

science and theology and between nations in a common task; namely, the building of a more humane culture. In as far as the Church becomes a support for the moral commitment of scientists, the Church can be seen as an ally of science.

In 1983 the same Pope spoke on the "Responsibility of Science."[11] Again he emphasized the ethical dimension of the scientific project. But he also addressed the question: What does the Church expect to get from science? He stated that we should not look to science to offer apologetic proofs for the truth of the church's teachings. Rather, the Church turns to science to "expand the horizon of its contemplation and of its admiration for the clarity with which the infinitely powerful God shines through His creation."

In the Fall 1987 an international research conference was convened at the Vatican Observatory at the request of the same Pope. Its purpose was to explore the current relations between theology and science. The hope of the scholars who met there was to make a move toward establishing a new level of discussion and mutual understanding between scientists, philosophers, and theologians. In 1989 the Pope addressed a letter to the director of the Vatican observatory on the occasion of the publication of the papers from that 1987 Study Week.[12] The papal message is a powerful appeal for the possibility and the urgency of a constructive relation between science and theology.

In this letter, the Pope describes the network of relations between the disciplines as a concern that is "crucial for the contemporary world." Both the Church and the scientific academies bear enormous responsibility for the human condition since both have been and still are major influences in the shaping of ideas and values that set the direction for the course of human action. The Pope asks theologians to take science with seriousness by attempting to integrate the findings of science within the context of their theological work.

Concerning the historical relation between the Church and science, the Pope recognizes that it has fluctuated in the past, at times taking a friendly form, at other times the form of hostility. This is the same Pope who lifted the condemnation of Galileo. Despite the pain of the past, the Pope suggests that there is a "growing critical openness" that characterizes the relation between religion and science. This is the sort of thing that can happen when two groups which at first seem to have nothing in common begin to enter into more congenial relations when they discover a common broader area of shared understanding and concern.

---

[11] "The Responsibility of Science," in: *The Pope Speaks* 28 (Fall 1983) 245–49.

[12] Russell, R.J., Stoeger, W.R., Coyne, G., eds. *Physics, Philosophy, and Theology: A Common Quest for Understanding* (Vatican City and Notre Dame, Ind.: Vatican Observatory and Notre Dame Press, 1988).

While the relation between religion and science is "still fragile and provisional," the Pope speaks of a movement toward a "more nuanced interchange" between them.

> We have begun to speak to one another on deeper levels than ever before, and with greater openness toward one another's perspectives. We have begun to search together for a more thorough understanding of one another's disciplines, with their competencies and their limitations, and especially for areas of common ground. In doing so, we have uncovered important questions which concern both of us, and which are vital to the larger human community we both serve. It is crucial that this common search based on critical openness and interchange should not only continue but also grow and deepen in its quality and scope.

Again, the Pope emphasizes what each has to offer for the movement of civilization and the world itself. Christianity offers a vision of "hope that the fragile goodness, beauty, and life we see in the universe is moving toward a completion and fulfillment which will not be overwhelmed by the forces of dissolution and death." Science offers knowledge of the processes and structures involved in the cosmos, and technology offers the means of employing that knowledge in ways that may either enhance life or finally destroy life and the environment that begets and sustains life. The situation in which we find ourselves points to the need to discover that sort of wisdom which will enable humanity to turn the ambiguous potential of technology into genuinely life-giving realities.

What the Pope envisions is not a fusion of science and theology into one discipline, for "religion is not founded on science nor is science an extension of religion. Each should possess its own principles, its pattern of procedures, its diversities of interpretation and its own conclusions." Rather than fusing the disciplines or making one subject to the other, the Pope speaks of an ongoing dialogue that recognizes the disciplinary autonomy of both sides of the dialogue, but envisions them as engaged in a common enterprise for the well-being of the human race. When the Pope speaks of religion, he extends his concern beyond the Christian religion and speaks of all the world's great religions. "We must ask ourselves whether both science and religion will contribute to the integration of human culture or to its fragmentation. It is a single choice, and it confronts us all. . . . Simple neutrality is no longer acceptable."

The concern of the papal statement may be put in the following way. In general, the Pope is concerned with building a friendly and constructive relation. Hence, we notice the lack of any stark, confrontational language. The statement emphasizes the autonomy of the disciplines, each having its own methodology, its own strong points and its own limitations. The relation suggested might be called one of critical correlation in the context of a larger problem: human destiny. Science offers the best available knowledge of how the world operates. Theology offers a vision of value, meaning, and hope. It would be a mistake to let either of these disciplines become the total picture. Theology should not look for scientific proofs for issues of faith. But it can look for insight into the nature of the world that it believes to be the world of God's creative activity. This is but a new version of the long-standing Christian vision of "faith seeking understanding."

VI) *Some Models*

The last few years have seen a number of significant publications dealing with the question of the relation between the world of science and the world of religion. In 1990 the first volume of Ian Barbour's Gifford Lectures entitled *Religion in an Age of Science* was published. The same year saw the publication of Nancey Murphy's *Theology in the Age of Scientific Reasoning* and W. Drees' *Beyond the Big Bang*. In 1993 A. Peacocke published *Theology for a Scientific Age*. J. Polkinghorne's Gifford Lectures appeared in 1994 under the title *The Faith of a Physicist*. This is just a small sampling of the serious work being done on the problem of the interface between the world of religion and that of the contemporary sciences. After so many years of neglect and outright warfare between these two worlds, it is significant to see so much excellent, serious discussion from the perspective of people deeply immersed in the sciences and others just as deeply involved in theological studies.

While books such as those just mentioned are addressed to a readership that is already reasonably literate in the sciences, John Haught's more recent book, *Science and Religion: From Conflict to Conversation,* is a remarkable attempt to reach a wider public. Haught has tried to offer a discussion of major questions which emerge for religion from the sciences in a way that is accessible not only to scientists, but to theologians, students, and other interested persons who may not have a detailed knowledge of science, and perhaps not even of theology. Haught's own modest hope is that the book might serve as "an introduction for non-experts."[13] Most recently, Haught has published a book entitled *God after Darwin: A Theology of Evolution.*[14] This is an exceptionally rich presentation of the sort of theological development that is possible by a theologian who is literate in the

---

[13] Haught, J., *Science and Religion: From Conflict to Conversation* (Mahwah, N.J.: Paulist Press, 1995) 2.

[14] Haught, J., *God after Darwin: A Theology of Evolution* (Boulder, Col.: Westview Press, 2000).

sciences and is willing to engage the scientific insights in a critical and creative way.

In speaking of religion, we consciously limit our remarks to Christianity. Much of this might be applicable also to Judaism and Islam. We leave that for others to decide. And to make any statements about the great religions of the East such as Taoism, Buddhism, and Hinduism would require a distinct study. Thus, when we speak of religion here, we have in mind Christianity, including not only its foundational experiences, but the reflective process that has given rise to great doctrinal systems.

Taking his orientation from recent studies such as those of Barbour and Drees on possible interfaces between the disciplines, Haught singles out four models for the relation between science and religion. These he calls: conflict, contrast, contact, confirmation. A few comments on each of these might be helpful for our discussion.

The conflict-model is one which makes it necessary to choose either science or religion to the exclusion of the other. This is probably the most familiar one since, as we have already indicated, so many people have grown up in modern, Western culture with the assumption that there is inevitably and necessarily a conflict between the claims of science and those of religion. While this model may well have its historical roots as far back as the Galileo-case, it is far from a dead issue even today. It operates from a basic sense of opposition that isolates the realm of religion from the work of the sciences. Those who opt for the sciences in this model often see "but one kind of knowledge; and one method for acquiring it" in the words of Thomas Huxley (1866). On the other hand, those who opt for religion often turn religion into a pseudo-science.

Barbour suggests that this conflict model is represented in a number of science writers in what he calls scientific materialism; and in biblical fundamentalists. Among scientific materialists he includes Steven Weinberg, Carl Sagan, Jacques Monod, and E. O. Wilson. Among biblical fundamentalists, he includes the New Right, the Moral Majority, and the so-called creation-science movement.

Second, there is the contrast-model. This model operates on the assumption that science and religion are two fundamentally different and unrelated realms of discourse. Science is informative and makes claims about objective reality. Religion, on the other hand, deals with the inner experience of the believer or the conduct of the worshiping community. Hence, there can really be no contradictions between them as long as one is clearly aware of the concerns and limits of each. Peace between religion and science is achieved, but only at the price of depriving religion of the claim of saying anything about the empirical world of ordinary experience.

Barbour describes this as a model of independence. Conflicts between science and religion can be avoided if the two enterprises are seen to be independent and autonomous. Each must keep off the other's turf. Each must tend to its own business and not meddle in the affairs of the other. In this model the two differ by virtue of contrasting methods, and contrasting language systems. L. Gilkey has suggested the following concerning the method question:

(1) Science seeks to explain objective, public, repeatable data; religion asks about order and beauty in the world and experiences in our inner life. (2) Science asks objective questions about *what* and *how;* religion asks personal *why-questions* about meaning and purpose and about our ultimate origin and destiny. (3) The basis of authority in science is logical coherence and experimental adequacy. The final authority in religion is God and revelation, understood through persons to whom enlightenment and insight were given, and validated in one's own experience. (4) Science makes quantitative predictions which can be tested experimentally; religion uses symbolic and analogical language to speak of the God which it believes to be transcendent.

This way of describing the two approaches was helpful in the context of the creation-science trials. It may, however, be applicable not only to the contrast model. It may be helpful in the contact model as well. But then it would lead to different conclusions.

Third, Haught speaks of the contact-model. This model moves from the conviction that science and theology are in fact looking at the same world, but they look through different lenses. Hence, while they do raise different kinds of questions, these questions are concerned with the same world. This means that the empirically-based positions of science may raise some serious questions for theology, and scientific discoveries may at some point require a significant redefinition of some very basic theological concepts and principles. But it also means that science must recognize the limitations of its own methodology. This model, therefore, leads one in the direction of conversation between the disciplines even while it attempts to avoid any form of reductionism or conflation of the disciplines. Its primary concern is the search for consonance and coherence. It is interested in how can one think theologically if, in fact, the scientific description of the cosmos is appropriate?

This model suggests that neither science nor religion should seek to dominate the other nor submit uncritically to the claims of the other. Yet each discipline should profit from and contribute to the attainments of the other. Both are needed together with other areas such as the arts to deal with the common, larger human problem: that of the meaning of life in the cosmos in which we are situated.

Barbour discusses the same approach under two distinct levels which he describes as dialogue and integration. By dialogue he means a range of indirect interactions between the two. Here he refers to the so-called boundary-questions. By this is meant that at its outer limits, science raises questions which it cannot answer precisely as science. He points out also some methodological parallels between the two disciplines. This involves the basic epistemological structures involved in both.

This level of interaction he distinguishes from a second which he calls integration. Under this name he discusses issues such as doctrinal reformulation and doctrinal synthesis done in the light of specific scientific insights and theories. This can take place at several levels. First, one can use scientific concepts as possible analogies for religious concerns. For example, the wave/particle language of quantum physics might be seen as analogous to the traditional paradoxical human/divine language used in theology to speak about Christ. Beyond this there is the possibility of restructuring the theological framework in relation to the scientific vision of an emerging cosmos. This would involve redefining some basic theological concepts in a new way. Many interested in doing this make use of some form of Process philosophy to carry out their project.

What is involved here might well be seen as the inner dynamic of the project of the great Scholastics of the Middle Ages. When confronted with a new world-view involving the entire corpus of Aristotle's writings (hence, physics, metaphysics, ethics, etc.), they chose not to reject it, but to engage it critically as a dialogue partner in constructing a new style of theology. But we must be aware that any such a synthesis is tentative and fragile, since the scientific vision involved is, by its very nature, tentative and incomplete. It is simply the best we can do at a given moment. Such an approach allows for the development of a world-view that integrates both the physical understanding of science with the vision of religious meaning into a larger road-map of reality. Many theologians would like to have something that seems more permanent. However, the apparent permanence of past formulations arises only because we tend to forget the historical circumstances in which such formulations came to be.

Finally, Haught makes a plea for something which he calls the confirmation-model. This moves from the conviction that there are ways in which religion, as understood in the Christian tradition, while not proving any specific scientific claims or theories, may in fact offer positive support for the scientific project as a whole. Religion, in the creative moments of its history, does not suppress the desire to know and understand, but encourages it. It is precisely the desire to know that is at work in the efforts of science. Hence, Haught concludes that there is something at least in the biblical tradition that encourages and supports the project of scientific investigation and research as such without confirming any specific result of such work.

Something like this argument has been made elsewhere, specifically about the role of the biblical tradition in Western history and culture. The basic claim is that this religious vision de-divinized the world with its basic conviction that the world is the world, and it is not God. Yet the tradition viewed the world as basically orderly and intelligible. Hence, the world could become the material for investigation and study. Hence, so the argument goes, the sciences as we know them have developed largely in the Western world, initially because the biblical vision opened the possibility of investigating the world. But the later working out of this project would involve an ongoing interaction between science and religion which at times has been painfully antagonistic.

It is good to keep in mind that religion gets its starting point neither from science nor from philosophy. But when religious consciousness arrives at a certain level of self-awareness, it can use critical thought processes to evaluate its own assumptions, and it can interact with the sciences of its time to develop a coherent world-view. We might think of science as a source of empirically-based knowledge about the *what* and *how* of the physical cosmos, and of religion as a source of values and wisdom in the light of which we might invest our existence in this sort of cosmos with a sense of meaning. Neither religion nor science alone can do this effectively. Both are needed in a project that is larger then either one of the disciplines in isolation

VII) *Conclusions*

From quite different sources we have seen an appeal for some form of conversation between theology and the sciences. This does not mean the same thing for all the authors we have cited. But, beginning with the papal statements and moving to those of serious authors in the field of science and religion, we find a search for areas of consonance and for some sense of a coherent world-view. We conclude this discussion with a summary statement of some of the basic assumptions that would be involved in such a discussion.

1) We might be led to ask why we should try to relate science and religion in such a dialogue? The answer lies in the area of our vision of human destiny and the future of humanity in this cosmos. Such a program would help provide a framework of values and a sense of meaning to the information presented by the sciences. Science describes *what* the cosmos is and

how the cosmos works. Theology attempts to discuss above all the question: *Why* it is at all?

2) Throughout this entire discussion, we must keep in mind that theology is not simply a matter of stating what are assumed to be revealed dogmas of faith. It is more than that in as far as it is a search for deeper understanding of the implications of the truths of faith. Theology, therefore, at some point attempts to develop systematic structures through which to communicate its sense of meaning. It is at this point that the relation between faith and reason becomes crucial. Any theological construct created today that engages the claims of the sciences will necessarily be incomplete and tentative. This is the unavoidable implication of the fact that our scientific knowledge of the world is incomplete and tentative. Hence any theological construct must share in that tentative character. This may be uncomfortable for certain understandings of what theology should be.

3) Theology should not look to science to prove the truth of its claims. Religion does not derive its vision from science, nor does it depend on science to prove its truth. A program of apologetics does not seem to be a helpful direction in which to move.

4) What, then, are we concerned with? We are concerned with seeing the possible coherence and concordance involved in the two visions. Here we are talking about the areas of cognitive harmony between science and theology. The hope is that the best insight from all areas of human experience—and religion is a form of human experience—might be brought together to provide a richer and more coherent picture of the world in which we live, and of ourselves as responsible ethical agents in this sort of world. Since for us this takes place after the so-called critical turn in Western experience, it will be much less pretentious in all of its claims about human knowledge. And it is particularly aware of the danger of religious dogmatism on the one side and of scientific dogmatism on the other.

We are looking for science not to prove the truth of religion, but to play a creative role together with religion and the arts in the construction of a relatively coherent vision of reality. We would want scholars of our time to do for us what the ancients and the medieval scholars did for their time: to create a road-map of reality to help guide us in our search for meaning. But we do this today with a deeper awareness that such road-maps are far more fragile than we have thought in the past.

5) What does the world look like when we view it in the light of contemporary insights? There are insights that cry out for reflection and understanding. From a scientific perspective, we see the cosmos as a unified, unfolding, unfinished chemical process that eventually brings forth life, consciousness, intelligence, and freedom at least on planet earth. And here

on planet earth, in the form of human intelligence, this cosmic process comes to ask about itself, about its ultimate source, and its ultimate goal or purpose, and how that purpose is to be attained. This vision, therefore, raises the question of origin and end, and the question of the moral consciousness that characterizes human existence in this sort of cosmos.

At present the most common cosmological model which scientists use to speak of this vision of an unfolding cosmos is known as the Big Bang model. We find this model pervasive in the scientific literature, where it appears with a number of variations that attempt to clarify the earliest stage of cosmic history. This issue includes a number of quantum-wave fluctuation theories at one end of the spectrum, usually attempting to account for the "first moment of time"; and the no-boundary theory at the other end of the spectrum, i.e., the more recent theory of S. Hawking which maintains there are no boundaries to space and time, hence no temporal beginning. We will discuss this matter more in later chapters. For the present, it is sufficient to indicate that the Big Bang model is not our direct concern. But we are concerned with the idea of the unfolding cosmos which the model attempts to clarify.

Our concern is not to prove any of the truths of faith, but to indicate (1) that there is not a contradiction between the two outlooks, i.e. science and Christian faith; (2) to search out what areas of coherence and consonance can be delineated between the two; and (3) to explore how we can think theologically about the issues of faith in the context of the cosmos as it is described in the light of the sciences.

2

The Vision of the Hebrew Scriptures

I) *The Genesis Texts*

When we are confronted with the biblical texts commonly associated with the theology of creation, current biblical scholarship calls on us to make an important decision about how to approach the Bible. If one sees the opening chapter of Genesis as a realistic description of the first six days of cosmic history, the conclusion seems unavoidable that there is a massive contradiction between the Bible and modern science. If, on the other hand, one approaches the biblical text through the insights of historical, textual criticism, the situation will be very different.

For those who take historical criticism as their guide, it is common to distinguish between the physical world-view that seems to stand behind the biblical texts and the religious message that the texts attempt to communicate. From the perspective of contemporary science, the physical world-view reflected in the texts is best described as archaic. But the religious message involved in the texts may yet be rich and important for human understanding. Also, among those who take historical criticism as a point of departure, it is common today to see the opening chapters of Genesis as coming from two different traditions. The older tradition, known as the Yahwist tradition because of the name it uses most commonly for God, is understood to begin with Genesis 2:4b. This tradition dates back to the tenth century B.C.E. The more recent tradition, known as the Priestly tradition because of the identity of its author or redactor, is dated at the time of the Babylonian Exile, that is around the sixth or fifth century B.C.E., or shortly thereafter. We shall comment first on the Priestly account and then on the Yahwist.

The Priestly account opens the book of Genesis in its present form. It is this account that begins with a description of the familiar six days of divine creative activity followed by the seventh day of divine blessing and rest (Gen 1:1–2:4a). The creative work of God is expressed with the Hebrew word *bara*. This word is used in the Bible only for divine activity, and it singles out such activity as unique and different from all creaturely activity. In this case, it is an activity which simply places a beginning for all that exists in the world. The author uses another metaphor for this divine activity; namely, the metaphor of divine speech. "Then God said: let there be . . ." and it came to be. The use of this metaphor of a commanding speech emphasizes the divine transcendence together with the personal character of God.

This remarkable text opens our vision to an orderly world that in its essence is declared by the Creator to be good; and, indeed, very good (Gen 1:31). One hears nothing of the matter/spirit dualism found in some Hellenistic philosophies and some Near Eastern religions. Creation is not just a question of spiritual existence; it is an issue of material existence as well. While humanity is deeply related to the rest of the created order, God has a particular aim for the human race. Humanity is created in the image and likeness of God.

> Then God said: "Let us make man in our image, after our likeness. . . ." So God created man in his image; in the divine image he created him; male and female he created them. God blessed them saying, "Be fertile and multiply; fill the earth and subdue it. Have dominion over the fish of the sea, the birds of the air, and all living things that move on the earth" (Gen 1:26-28).

According to the wide consensus of contemporary exegetes, this is probably best seen not as a statement of the essence of human nature, but as a statement of a function. It points to humanity's relation to all other living creatures and to the earth as a whole. Human beings are intimately interwoven with the rest of the created order. The role of humanity is to live in such a way that the loving creativity of God will become manifest within the created order through human relations with other humans and with the non-human world. The life-style of humans should reflect in the world the loving, creative care of God for all of creation.

It has been common over the years to interpret the text we have just cited in such a way that the image of God referred only to the male. Contemporary exegesis commonly argues that this is inaccurate, and that the function of the divine image refers to both the male and the female. Both share in the same divinely given task with respect to the created order.

The Priestly account reaches its highpoint with the symbolism of the seventh day. God has finished the work of creation and now rests on the seventh day. "So God blessed the seventh day and made it holy, because on it God rested from all the work that had been done in creation" (Gen 2:3).

This may be seen as a legitimation of the Jewish practice of Sabbath required by the Torah in as far as this practice may now be seen to be rooted in the very origins of the world and inaugurated by the Creator God of the entire world. Torah belongs to the very structure of creation. This may be seen also as a reminder to the people of their obligations to God the Creator symbolized by the Sabbath, for those who live according to the Torah live in harmony with the primal order according to which God has created the world.

The Yahwist account beginning in Genesis 2 is very different. While the Priestly tradition seems to be concerned primarily with the creative relation of God to the world and to all in it, and with humanity's place in the world, the Yahwist tradition seems to be primarily concerned with the failure of humanity to live up to its God-given task. There is a wide-spread agreement among exegetes that the point of departure for the writing of the material in the Yahwist account is not the experience of some eye-witness of the beginnings of human history. It is, rather, the present experience of the writer reflecting on the mystery of human experience as he finds it in his own time and place.

Assuming that the author is a member of the Jewish people, we can envision him to be reflecting not only on his personal experience, but on the experience of his people over the centuries. From this perspective he lays out what may be seen as a description of the polarities of human history not only as they may be seen in the case of the Hebrew people, but as they may be seen in human history as a whole. From this perspective it would be misleading to look to these texts as sources of information about some paradisal situation at the beginning of history.

While the description of the creation of humanity in the first chapter seems to emphasize the dignity of humankind, the text of the second chapter describes humanity graphically in terms of the earthy roots through which humanity is tied to the earth. God is here described as an artist fashioning a human form from the clay of the ground and breathing into it the breath of life (Gen 2:7).

The play on words seen in the Hebrew text is lost in any translation. For in Hebrew the word for ground is *adamah* and the name of that which is formed from the ground is *adam*. It appears that Adam is not first of all a proper name, but a description of the earthy roots of humanity. It might be fair to see this as a way of modifying the temptation to over-state the exalted dignity of humanity suggested in the first chapter. It can be seen also in relation to what is said later: "The Lord God took the man and settled him in the garden of Eden to cultivate and care for it" (Gen 2:15).

The text goes on to describe how God surrounded Adam with all sorts of animal life, since it is not good for him to be alone. When none of these animals proves to be a suitable partner for the man, God then formed the woman from the rib of the man (Gen 2:21ff.). What is described as the failure of Adam and Eve is best seen not as something that happened once and for all at the outset of human history, but rather as something that is always present in human experience. And Genesis 3 is best read in the wider context of the biblical text up to Genesis 11. The failure of Adam and Eve is described as a failure to deal with limits appropriately. From there, we see the history of humanity as one of mistrust, fratricide, enmity, and discord. Humans find it hard to deal with the other and have a driving tendency to push beyond appropriate limits. The description leads us to the disaster of the flood. The story of Noah leads to a covenant in which the fidelity of God is symbolized with the cosmic sign of the rainbow. From there, the text takes us quickly to the building of the tower of Babel, that eloquent symbol of human pride that leads to the wide-spread division of people and their inability to communicate in a healthy way.

Instead of looking at this narrative as a source of information about specific individuals and events, it might be more helpful to envision it as the overture to an opera. As a well-crafted overture either sets the general mood or actually lays out the principle themes and characters of the opera that is to follow, so the biblical text lays out the basic themes that are constantly enacted throughout human history. The real intent of the text is not to describe specific events and particular individuals of the past. It is, rather, to describe the present situation of humanity as a whole. Humanity is taken from the earth, but is called to a noble destiny. From the beginning, however, humanity has failed by pushing beyond the limits of human nature in the desire to make humans the final arbiters of good and evil. But even in the face of human failure, God does not desert creation. The promise of Gen 3:15 will eventually be seen as the protoevangelium; the first announcement of a savior.

Thus, if we read the text as a unit from Genesis 1 to Genesis 11, we discover a remarkable, dramatic movement. The text begins with a vision of the fundamental harmony of the order of creation; the creative action of God brings order out of chaos. Humanity is integrated into the world in many ways. Rooted in the earth, humanity is called to a God-given responsibility for the good of the whole. We have then seen this juxtaposed with the violent disruption of that order and a near-return to chaos through inappropriate human interventions. Finally, in the story of Noah we discover a new creation placed under the cosmic sign of the rainbow as the sign of God's everlasting covenant with creation. From here the text moves through a list of genealogies on to the account of Babel, and then quickly to the call of Abraham. The overture has been completed. Now the drama of patriarchal history will begin.

II) *Prophetic Reflection*

A major theme that stands out in the prophetic tradition is the conviction that the creative power of God manifests itself in a dramatic way in the history of Israel. The God who has created them as a people, who has liberated them from Egypt, and who is with them as a saving presence in their journey to the Promised Land is the Creator God who has called the whole of reality into existence and sustains it as its creative Ground. This Creator God is with Israel even in the tragedy of the Babylonian Exile and through the mouth of the prophets promises liberation anew and restoration of the people in its homeland. The creative power of YHWH is contrasted sharply with the impotence of the gods.

> Thus says the Lord, Israel's King and redeemer, the Lord of hosts: "I am the first and I am the last; there is no God but me. Who is like me? Let him stand and speak, make it evident, and confront me with it . . . . Is there a God or any Rock besides me? Idol makers all amount to nothing, and their precious works are of no avail, as they themselves give witness . . . . Indeed, all the associates of anyone who forms a god, or casts an idol to no purpose, will be put to shame; they will all assemble and stand forth, and will be reduced to fear and shame" (Isa 44, 6-10).

The prophetic vision uses all the language and symbolism of the Mosaic experience to envision the future. This is particularly clear in Deutero-Isaiah and Trito-Isaiah (Isa 40-66). We see here a typological correspondence between beginning of Israel's history as a people and end of history, now projected in rich eschatological imagery. There will be a new creation, and the law will be written on the flesh of human hearts and not on tablets of stone. Behind this movement is the movement to the high monotheism of later Judaism. The God of this people is eventually seen as the God of all creation and of all people.

By creating Israel anew out of the chaos of the Exile, God reveals the original divine power to create order out of chaos. Creation language serves as the language to speak of the restored Israel (Isa 62:1-12). It serves also to evoke the vision of a future which will be a "new creation," "new heavens and a new earth" that brings God's world to its final perfection (Isa 65:17ff). With this we see how the biblical vision looks to the future fulfillment as the goal of God's creative activity.

The vision of a future fulfillment would be taken up by the apocalyptic literature. Here one looks forward to a dramatic conflict between the powers of evil and the power of good. In the eschatological victory of God, the power of evil will be definitively broken. The present age of turmoil in the old creation will give way to a new age of peace and harmony in the new creation.

III) *Wisdom and Psalms*

If the material we have discussed above is concerned extensively with the mystery of salvation and the history of God's saving interaction with the Hebrew people, the Wisdom literature, while not ignoring the question of salvation (Psalm 78; Wisdom 10; 11), shifts the readers attention more to the religious significance of the world of God's creation. In the context of religious systems which tend to divinize the cosmos, or particular things within the cosmos, the authors of the biblical texts are concerned with emphasizing that, for all the beauty and wonder of the created order, the world is not divine. Rather, its beauty points to an even richer beauty in the reality of God who is the Creator of the world, but not a part of the world. From this perspective, we might understand the great hymns of praise found in the psalms. "The earth is the Lord's and all that is in it; the world and those who live there. For God founded it on the seas and established it over the rivers" (Psalm 24:1-2). And: "By the Lord's word the heavens were made; by the breath of his mouth all their host . . . Let all the earth fear the Lord; let all who dwell in the world show reverence. For he spoke, and it came to be, commanded, and it stood in place" (Psalm 33:6, 8-9).

The whole of Psalm 104 is a sustained eulogy of God the Creator. The author relates the creative action of God to all dimensions of the world. Full of wonders as it is, yet the world is not God. "How manifold are your works, O Lord! In wisdom you have wrought them all—the earth is full of your creatures . . . May the glory of the Lord remain forever; may the Lord be glad in his works" (Psalm 104:24, 31).

Of particular significance for our reflections is the way in which the development of wisdom reflections eventually lead to a personification of wisdom. The book of Wisdom offers an outstanding example of this in its eulogy of wisdom.

> For Wisdom is mobile beyond all motion, and she penetrates and pervades all things by reason of her purity. For she is an aura of the might of God and a pure effusion of the glory of the Almighty; therefore nought that is sullied enters into her. For she is the refulgence of eternal light, the spotless mirror of the power of God, the image of his goodness. And she,

who is one, can do all things, and renews everything while herself per-during" (Wisdom 7:24-27).

The book of Proverbs offers a moving reflection on wisdom.

> The Lord begot me, the firstborn of his ways, the forerunner of his prodi-gies of long ago. From of old I was poured forth . . . When he estab-lished the heavens I was there, when he marked out the vault over the face of the deep; when he made firm the skies above, when he fixed fast the foundations of the earth; when he set for the sea its limit so that the waters should not transgress his command. Then was I beside him as his craftsman, and I was the Lord's delight day by day, playing before him all the while, playing on the surface of the earth; and I found delight in the sons of men" (Prov 8:22-31).

In this literature the focus is more on the present beauty and magnifi-cence of the created world, and not so much on the historical acts of God as Israel's savior as we noted in the prophetic material. It is not hard to under-stand why Jewish Rabbinic commentators tended to identify Wisdom with the "beginning" of Gen 1:1, in which God created all things. This in turn will shed light on Paul's christology, and the tendency to connect Wisdom with the incarnation of the Word, and thus to see Christ as involved in crea-tion "from the beginning." The same can be said of the prologue of John's Gospel. We will discuss this in more detail in the next chapter.

IV) *Conclusion*

As we look over all of this Scriptural material, we can say that, granted the distinction between the religious message of the Scriptures and the physical world-view within which it is projected, the message is rich and profound. The historical-prophetic material amounts to a challenge to trust in the goodness and love of the Creator God and the work of creation de-spite the pain and trials of human history. The Wisdom tradition is a sus-tained call to sing the praises of the Creator for the great work of creation.

Clearly the physical vision of the world involved here is often mythical and archaic in character. If we focus our attention on the concrete details of the diverse accounts, we will find it impossible to come to a unified pic-ture. For example, the Priestly account describes the creation of the world-order and all its inhabitants, and finally presents the creation of humanity. The Yahwist, on the other hand, describes the creation of humanity, and then describes God creating the beings that are to surround humanity. If these are to be taken as accounts of natural history, they can hardly be har-monized. Yet the redactor of the present text places the two accounts in immediate juxtaposition. It is hard to avoid the conclusion that the real intention of the redactor is to convey a message other than the concrete details of the stories. If we follow the insight of St. Augustine, physics is not the message of the Bible. The real point of the texts is a religious message which offers insight into the meaning of existence. It is a sustained effort to encourage humanity to take up existence with a sense of gratitude and praise of the Creator.

In this case, it follows that if the message of the Bible is not about the physical details of creation at its beginning, then the insights of science concerning cosmic origins need not be seen as contradicting the message of the Bible.

As regards the religious vision, the following points can be singled out:

1) God is viewed as sovereignly free, creative power who is the source of order in the world.

2) The creative activity of God embraces the world from the beginning to the end of its history.

3) The created world is in essence good.

4) Humanity has a special role to play in this world of God's creation.

5) While the physical view of the world is that of a static order reflecting God's stability and fidelity, the biblical vision sees a dynamic vision of history as the interplay between divine freedom and human freedom.

6) The problem of evil enters the picture primarily in the form of moral failure through the activity of human beings.

7) With that moral evil, human beings find themselves at odds with one another and with the world around them in as far as they are at odds with God.

8) Salvation is, in essence, the completion of God's creative work with the world and humanity.

3

Creation in the Christian Scriptures

The Christian understanding of creation is not based simply on the repetition of the texts of Genesis nor on other material from the Hebrew Scriptures. There is a development of insight in the Christian Scriptures parallel to that found in the history of the Hebrew Bible. The Christian authors, of course, have the centuries of Jewish reflection to draw from. But gradually they come to reflect on the mystery of creation from the perspective of their own experience of salvation in Jesus Christ. At this level there emerges a specifically Christian understanding of the mystery of creation.

I) *The Synoptic Gospels*

It is commonly argued that the Synoptic Gospels present little if any explicit reflection on what might be called a theology of creation. Much less would they provide any material that would expressly relate the Christian experience of Christ with any form of creation-theology. On the other hand, a careful reading of these Gospels would certainly suggest that they presuppose much of the vision that the Hebrew traditions offered for an understanding of the world. In the light of the best knowledge available about the actual ministry of Jesus, it seems possible to see a number of ways in which Jesus related his ministry to the creative work of YHWH. The following might serve as examples.

1) It is commonly recognized among biblical scholars that the metaphor of the Kingdom of God played a basic role in the preaching and ministry of Jesus. The Kingdom metaphor is related to the Jewish expectations of the

future fulfillment of God's promise. When this metaphor is viewed in the context of its interpretation through parables and miracle stories, the implication of a deep relation between the created order and the understanding of salvation is clear.

2) Jesus used a wide range of examples from the world of nature and from the every-day experience of the people to communicate his understanding of the Kingdom: the seed sown on different kinds of ground; the weeds growing with the wheat; the mustard seed; the work in the vineyard; the lost sheep and the Good Shepherd; the preparation of bread. All these appear as means of opening his listeners to the mystery of the Kingdom.

3) The tradition of the healings is particularly significant. Healings of the body suggest an understanding of wholeness and salvation that differs significantly from Hellenistic ideas of the body/soul complex. The God of Jesus is interested not only in souls, but in people and in all that makes up their existence.

The God that is communicated through the ministry of Jesus is a God of care and concern for all of creation, even for the smallest and apparently insignificant things and people. Thus, while we do not find an extensive or explicit development of creation theology, we do see that the ministry and preaching of Jesus depends deeply on the Hebrew tradition of creation. Having said this, it remains to be said that a very different form of reflection will be found in the writings of Paul and John, and the Epistle to the Hebrews.

II) *The Pauline Epistles*

Paul speaks of the God "who gives life to the dead, and calls into being what does not exist" (Rom 4:17). He thus identifies the God of Christian faith who has raised Jesus from the dead with the God of creation. In the same epistle Paul reflects the Wisdom tradition in his argument concerning the guilt of the pagans. They should have been able to come to an appropriate knowledge of God that would guide them in their life, but they did not do so.

> Since the creation of the world, invisible realities such as God's eternal power and divinity, have become visible, recognized through the things God has made. Therefore these people have no excuse. For though they certainly had knowledge of God, they did not glorify him as God nor give thanks to God. . . . (Rom 1:20-21).

The created order reveals God so that all may come to know God. The Wisdom tradition had maintained that human beings were capable of attaining wisdom to the extent that they were capable of discerning the order of created things. The wise person is one who accepts and lives in accordance with that divinely given order. The pagans, in the mind of Paul, have not done this. Instead they have created false idols of creatures and have given themselves to all manner of perversity. They have no excuse, says Paul.

To learn how to discern the true meaning of creation as a revelation of God is wisdom. To turn the good creatures of God into idols that replace God in human life is to allow the world to take on a demonic power over human life and to turn human, spiritual endeavor away from the only God, who is the Creator of all. It is to invest the limited good of creation with the absolute good of the divine. This is a failure to find true wisdom. The result of this is a distortion of human relations to the created world in a form that is ultimately destructive. This theme will persist over the centuries in the history of Christian spirituality.

In the case of the other Pauline literature, Christ is given a role that extends from creation to the final consummation of creation in the Kingdom of God. Already in the First Epistle to the Corinthians we find a text that relates Christ to creation. "For us there is one God, the Father, from whom all things come and for whom we exist; and one Lord Jesus Christ, through whom all things come, and through whom we exist" (1 Cor 8:6). The prepositions *from* and *for* point to the Father as source and goal of creation. The preposition *through* points to Christ in terms of some form of instrumentality or mediation. In as far as all things are made through him, he is connected with creation. In as far as we live through him, he mediates salvation to creation.

Other writings in the Pauline tradition develop the christological orientation found already in the texts just cited. The Epistle to the Ephesians raises the idea of election in Christ: "He chose us in him (= Christ) before the foundation of the world, to be holy and without blemish before him. In love he destined us for adoption to himself through Jesus Christ . . ." (Eph 1:4-5). The same epistle speaks of the cosmic role of Christ in the metaphor of recapitulation. In Christ, God gives the cosmos a Head under which it is unified and set in order. God's plan is: ". . . to sum up all things in Christ, in heaven and on earth" (Eph 1:10).

A particularly powerful example of this sort of reflection is found in the great hymn of Colossians:

> He is the image of the invisible God, the first-born of all creatures. For in him were created all things in heaven and on earth, the visible and the invisible, whether thrones or dominations, or principalities or powers; all things were created through him and for him. He is before all things, and

> in him all things hold together. He is head of the body, the church; he is the beginning, the first born from the dead, so that in all things he himself might be preeminent. For in him all the fullness was pleased to dwell, and through him to reconcile all things for him, making peace through the blood of his cross (through him), whether those on earth or those in heaven (Col 1:15-20).

This text is the source for what later theologians will call the doctrine of the absolute predestination of Christ. That is, if we ask those theologians why God has created the universe their response will be the following. God has created so that the sort of union between God and creation may take place which Christians believe has taken place in Christ. God creates so as to bestow the riches of life and love on others and so that creatures may find their fulfillment in a loving union with God. This is what Christians believe has taken place in the person of Christ. Here the question about our ultimate origins is given a specifically Christian answer. We might conclude from such texts that the figure of Christ is not extrinsic to the universe. In fact, we might say that God's creative action reaches a high point in the relation between world and God in the one whom Christians call the Christ.

While we believe, in line with such texts, that the mystery of the ground of our being has been communicated in a distinctive manner in the history and person of Jesus, yet there is the abiding sense that this Christian revelation does not abrogate a more primal revelation of God in the cosmos itself. As we have seen above in the text from Romans, the God who creates can be encountered in our experience of the created universe. And the God we find there is the same God we meet in Jesus Christ.

III) *The Epistle to the Hebrews*

The Jewish tradition of wisdom seems to be the backdrop for the vision of this Christian text. Wisdom is God's agent; hence it is to be thought of as personal and not as a mere idea. Wisdom becomes incarnate in Jesus. God creates through the Son who is the exact image of the Father, and who brings God's revelation to its fullness. If God is the ultimate ground of creation, God works through an agent. And that agent, spoken of in the Hebrew tradition as wisdom, is here named the Son of God.

> In times past, God spoke in partial and various ways to our ancestors through the prophets; in these last days, he spoke to us through a son whom he made heir of all things, and through whom he created the universe, who is the refulgence of his glory, the very imprint of his being, and who sustains all things by his mighty word. When he had accom-

plished purification from sins, he took his seat at the right hand of the
Majesty on high, as far superior to the angels as the name he has inherited
is more excellent than theirs (Heb 1:1-4).

The text presents the Son from three perspectives. The eternal Son is active in creation. The incarnate Son is the definitive bearer of revelation and
the agent of salvation. The glorified Christ sits at the "right hand of the
Majesty." If the activity of God that calls the world into being is the same
as that which communicates to us in the life and ministry of Christ, then
both creation and redemption are mysteries of divine revelation or divine
self-communication. It is one and the same Son who is mediator of both.
Hence both are intimately related as mysteries of salvation.

IV) *The Prologue of the Fourth Gospel*

The opening of the Fourth Gospel takes the reader back to the opening
lines of Genesis, particularly if we look at both texts in their Greek form.
The Septuagint Greek translation of Genesis begins: *en arche . . .* The
Greek text of the Fourth Gospel begins with exactly the same words. The
text of Genesis goes on to describe God's creative activity not in terms of
what we have come to think of as creation from nothing, but in terms of the
divine action that, in sovereign freedom and power, brings order out of
chaos. The Hebrew text had used the word *tohu va bohu* to express what
we call chaos. A current English translation reads as follows: "In the beginning when God created the heavens and the earth, the earth was a formless void, and darkness covered the face of the deep, while a wind from
God swept over the face of the waters" (Gen 1:1-2). The beginning of the
Fourth Gospel can be read in juxtaposition with the text of Genesis:

> In the beginning was the Word, and the Word was with God, and the
> Word was God. . . . All things came to be through him, and without him
> nothing came to be. What came to be through him was life. . . . And the
> Word became flesh and made his dwelling among us (John 1:1-14).

Could it be that John is rewriting the opening of Genesis in the light of the
Christian experience of Jesus Christ? Creation is a movement from chaos
to cosmos, and the order that is characteristic of the cosmos is mediated
through the eternal Word of God who became enfleshed in Jesus of
Nazareth.

From the perspective of these elements of the Christian Scriptures, it
follows that early in the Christian tradition the biblical writers express the
conviction that we encounter the eternal ground of our existence as it has
become enfleshed in the history of Jesus Christ. The mystery of Christ,

therefore, pertains to the specifically Christian doctrine of creation. We will discuss this later in some detail when we look at the historical development of the doctrine.

V) *The New Creation*

The close connection between the mystery of creation and that of salvation is indicated in the scriptural use of the language about a new creation and a new humanity to designate salvation (Gal 6: 15; 2 Cor 5:17; Rom 6:4; Eph 2:15; 4:24; Col 3:10). The idea is found already in Paul's use of the Adam-Christ parallel (Rom 5:12-19; 1 Cor 15:45). Adam stands at the beginning of the old creation; Christ, the new Adam, stands at the beginning of the new creation. The cross of Christ opens the way to the new creation which is revealed above all in the mystery of the resurrection.

To understand salvation as a new creation does not mean that we destroy the meaning and value of creation itself. Rather, it means seeing creation in its proper relationship to its goal. If the end of the first creation is seen to reside in glorifying God, the mystery of Christ appears as the highest realization of that glorification (Phil 2:5-11; John 13:32; 14:13; 17:4).

If this new creation points ultimately to the eschatological fulfillment of God's creative aim, within history it is to take the form of a genuine life in Christ (John 5:26; 6:48; 14:6; 1 John 1:2; 5:11). This would involve a new unity of humankind (Eph 2:14) in which human beings will put on a new self "which is being renewed, for knowledge, in the image of its creator" (Col 3:10).

The final goal toward which the history of creation and grace is moving is elicited in Scripture with the language of the new heaven and the new earth. This is particularly the case in the book of Revelation.

> Then I saw a new heaven and a new earth. The former heaven and the former earth had passed away, and the sea was no more. I also saw the holy city, a new Jerusalem, coming down out of heaven from God, prepared as a bride adorned for her husband. I heard a loud voice from the throne saying: "Behold, God's dwelling is with the human race. He will dwell with them, and they will be his people, and God himself will always be with them as their God. He will wipe every tear from their eyes, and there shall be no more death or mourning, wailing or pain, (for) the old order has passed away" (Rev 21:1-4).

The overtones of the Jewish Exodus-experience and the covenant are unmistakable. The covenant formula was: I will be your God; you will be my people. During the wandering in the desert, the tent was the place in which the sacred artifacts of the covenant were kept. The tent of the desert experience anticipates the function of the temple yet to be built in Jerusalem. It was this same word that appears in the prologue to John's Gospel to name God's dwelling place in the form of the incarnate Word. Here it is in the description of the final fulfilling relation between God and creation.

The idea of a radical renewal had already appeared in the Hebrew prophets (Isa 65:17; 66:22). In the Christian Scriptures this renewal is seen to take place in the power of Christ who has broken the power of forces of evil (1 Cor 15:20-28), has established the messianic reign, and has subjected himself to the Father. Here the goal of the original creation is realized as humanity is drawn with Christ into the divine rest which had been foreshadowed in the Sabbath Rest of Genesis.

VI) *Conclusion*

From the above, it can be concluded that the Christian Scriptures present no single view of the created world. Nor is there a clear, distinctive physical cosmology. As had been the case with the Hebrew Scriptures, when a physical world-view is discernible behind the texts, it is commonly that of the non-biblical culture in which the authors of the Scriptures found themselves. In the world of antiquity, this would most often be a rather static concept of the world as the stage on which the dynamism of the history of salvation is enacted.

A number of strong themes can be high-lighted. (1) In both the Hebrew Scriptures and the Christian Scriptures, there is the abiding conviction that a good, loving, and faithful God is the ultimate ground of the world; and that therefore the world of creation is fundamentally good. (2) Both the Hebrew and the Christian traditions point out that the world, though at root good, can gain a demonic power over human beings. (3) Particularly the Wisdom literature of the Hebrew Scriptures and the christological reflections of the Christian Scriptures suggest that the world of creation can teach us that there is a God to reach for in the human, spiritual journey. (4) For Christian reflection, it becomes important to see that the mystery of Christ pertains to the very structure of creation and its history. It is in Christ that creation finds the anticipation of its eschatological fulfillment.

From all of this, it may be concluded that the Christian theology of creation is badly misconstrued if it is seen as a description of the first physical events of cosmic history, or if it is seen as a sort of philosophical ontology adorned with a few theological decorations. From a scriptural perspective, the purpose and meaning of creation is to make possible the covenant between God and humanity which finds its highest realization in Christ. Creation-faith, then, is above all the recognition of the absolute power of the God who is met in history. This God is not one among many, but the one, absolute ground of all reality. The question that lies behind the scriptural theology of creation is the basic question of the meaning of existence as that question comes to conscious awareness in the history of the Jewish and the Christian people. The scriptural response to that question will carry the theology of creation into the doctrine of salvation and eschatological completion.

4

Creation from Nothing

Contemporary physicists and cosmologists often speak of the "nothing" from which the cosmos springs. We need only think of the many summary articles that appeared in the news media in the 1980s when the new cosmology made front-page news for a while, and scientists were being quoted about many issues. Or we can think of Edward Tryon who, when asked how the universe came to be, replied: "It's just one of those things that happen from time to time."[1] There is a chapter at the end of Alan Guth's *The Inflationary Universe* entitled "A Universe Ex Nihilo."[2] Richard Morris, a physicist and well-known author, asks in *Cosmic Questions*, "What is nothing like?" In describing what he calls the new field of quantum cosmology as of 1993, Morris says: "Theories of nothingness have become an important part of cosmology in the last few years."[3] He is here discussing above all various theories of quantum fluctuations.

This is first a linguistic issue. At this level, it can be confusing since, historically, the idea of creation from nothing has its roots in Christian theology. In that theological context, it came to take on a specific, technical meaning. The issue can best be clarified by looking at some of the history that gave rise to the term. After the linguistic issue is clarified, there then arises a more basic question: Why is there anything at all, when there seems to be no need for it to be?

[1] Cfr. Alan Guth, *The Inflationary Universe: The Quest for a New Theory of Cosmic Origins* (Reeding, Mass.: Addison-Wesley Publ. Co., 1997) 12–14.
[2] Guth, *op. cit.,* 271ff.
[3] Richard Morris, *Cosmic Questions: Galactic Halos, Cold Dark Matter, and the End of Time* (New York: John Wiley & Sons, 1993) 125ff.

I) *Greek Thought and the Biblical Sources*

It has commonly been thought that the doctrine of creation from nothing is contained in the opening lines of Genesis. More recent critical studies suggest that this theological idea is not really the point of this particular text. The concept of creation from nothing is the fruit of ongoing discussion of Christianity with alternate world-views, both mythological and philosophical, in the world of antiquity. This interaction gives rise to the concept of creation from nothing with a particular metaphysical understanding of being which would not have been in the mind of the author of the biblical text.

"Nothing arises from nothing." Thus wrote Melissus of Samos in the fifth century B.C.E. Later Aristotle would describe this view as the common opinion of the philosophers. But, if nothing comes from nothing, yet something exists, how are we to understand this? One solution for the world of ancient philosophy was to conclude that the world was, in fact, eternal. As we know, this was the view of Aristotle, and it would become the object of much discussion in theological circles of the thirteenth century.

It was not uncommon to think of the origin of the present universe through the organization of pre-existent matter, perhaps through the operation of a Demiurge, as we find it in Plato's *Timaeus*. In non-biblical religious traditions, it was not unusual to think of the origin of the world through the work of two basic principles; one a principle of goodness, the other a principle of evil. This might offer an explanation for the existence of good and evil in the present form of the world. Or one might think of the origin of the world through the relation between a female and a male divinity; an earth-mother and a sky-god, for example.

Against such a diversity of views, the early Fathers of Christianity eventually forged the idea of creation from nothing. In the world of the Fathers, this amounted to breaking out of the Hellenistic forms cosmology mentioned above. If we were to ask about a Scriptural basis for this concept, a likely place would be a text from the second book of the Maccabees. There, the mother of the Maccabees is encouraging her son in the face of his impending death at the hand of the king. She says: "I beg you, child, look at the heavens and the earth and see all that is in them; then you will know that God did not make them out of existing things; and in the same way the human race came into existence" (2 Macc 7:28).

Some contemporary biblical scholars see this as the first biblical mention of a creation from nothing. Others are quick to point out that even though the text sounds like a creation from nothing, it would not have been understood in the ontological sense that the term would later acquire in Christian usage. To its original author, this text may well have meant something similar to the opening of Genesis; namely, a shaping of what had been chaos into an orderly world. It is interesting, however, to view the issue with the Greek text in mind. There the crucial phrase "not out of existing things" appears in the Greek formulation οὐκ ἐξ ὄντων. This was seen by early Christian writers and translators as an explicit statement of creation from nothing.

A very early example of this Christian interpretation is found in the text known as the *Shepherd of Hermas* (ca. 150 C.E.). This speaks of: "The God who dwells in the heavens and created what is from what is not, and increased and multiplied it for the sake of God's holy church . . ." (*Vision*, 1, 6).[4] Later in the same work we read the following: "First of all believe that God is one, who created everything and maintained it, and who made everything to be out of what was not, who contains everything but alone is not contained" (*Mandate* 1,1).[5]

Thus we see that there is very early evidence for a Christian understanding of creation from nothing even though there may be no unambiguous evidence for the idea in the Scriptures. This is understandable if we keep in mind that the biblical text we have cited uses the participle of the verb ειναι which in Greek means simply *to be*. And the passage under consideration is using a cognate form of that word. If all one sees is the Greek text, and if one is familiar with Greek philosophy, one can understandably conclude that the text could be taken to mean creation from nothing. In a similar passage, the Epistle to the Romans speaks of God's actions as that of a God "who gives life to the dead and calls into being what does not exist" (Rom 4:17).

Again we are confronted with participial forms of the verb for *to be*. God makes things to be which had not been (μή ὄντα ὡς ὄντα). The context in this case has to do with belief in the resurrection and not with any explicit theology of the origin of the world. But if resurrection is understood to be a new creation, the text might be seen as a call to trust in that creative power which is strong enough to restore the dead to life.

In Western Christian theology, the insights of Augustine would be of far-reaching significance down to the present. He clearly reflects the idea of creation from nothing. But his theology of creation reflects an obvious, unresolved tension between the biblical sense of the goodness even of material reality and the neo-Platonic sense that material being and multiplicity is as close to nothing as it is possible to get and yet to exist. We hear this in a text of the *Confessions:*

---

[4] *The Shepherd of Hermas,* commentary by Carolyn Osiek, in *Hermeneia Series* (Minneapolis: Fortress Press, 1999) 41.

[5] *Op. cit.,* 103.

> In the beginning, which is of you, in your Wisdom, which is born of your own substance, you created something, and that something you created from nothing. You did not make heaven and earth out of yourself, for then they would have been equal to your Only-Begotten, and through this equal also to you. But in no way was it right that anything which was not of you should be equal to you. There was nothing beyond you from which you might make them, O God, one Trinity and threefold Unity. Therefore you created heaven and earth out of nothing; a great thing and a little thing. For you are almighty and good, to make all things good, the great heaven and the little earth. You were, and there was naught else out of which you made heaven and earth; two beings, one near to you, the other near to nothingness; one to which you alone would be superior, the other to which nothing would be inferior.[6]

We note in this text the way in which *the beginning* relates to the origin of Wisdom within God. It is, in fact, the begetting of the second person of the Trinity within the mystery of the divine. In his work on the Trinity, Augustine will treat this explicitly as a form of immanent, intellectual emanation within God. In this sense the way in which the Son is from the Father is distinguished from the way in which creation is from God. It is very clear in this text that the God who is good creates out of nothing. And *all things* that the good God creates are also good. This includes both heaven and earth. But hardly has he said this than he goes on to say that, while heaven is close to God, earth is close to nothing. The sense of Plotinian emanationism is unmistakable here, and with it the distrust of materiality. Thus, this text gives expression to a tension that will remain in Christian neo-Platonism well into the Middle Ages and beyond and will become a common element in Christian spirituality.

Closely connected with the concept of creation from nothing in the thought of Augustine is the concept of a creation in time. It will be recalled that among the ancient Greek philosophers, the sense that the basic elements that make up creation as we know it today would be understood to have existed forever, perhaps not in their present form, but in some way nonetheless. The early Christian Fathers rejected these views and replaced them with the distinction between the eternity of God and the temporal character of the created world. Augustine gave eloquent expression to this Christian view. The created world, and humanity within it, must have a beginning in time, since only God is eternal, without beginning or end.

> The distinguishing mark between time and eternity is the fact that the former does not exist without some movement and change while in the case of the latter there is no change at all. . . . Now, since God, in whose

---

[6] *Confessions* 12, 7, tr. John K. Ryan (New York: Image, 1960) 308–09.

eternity there is absolutely no change, is the Creator and Ruler of time, I do not see how we can say that God created the world after a space of time had elapsed unless we admit also that previously some creature had existed whose movements would mark the course of time. Again, sacred and infallible Scripture tells us that in the beginning God created heaven and earth in order. Now, unless this means that nothing had been made before, it would have been stated that whatever else God had made before was created in the beginning. Undoubtedly, then, the world was made not in time but together with time. For, what is made in time is made after one period of time and before another; that is, after a past and before a future time. But there could have been no past time, since there was nothing created by whose movements and change time could be measured. The fact is that the world was made simultaneously with time, if with creation motion and change began.[7]

From this discussion, we might conclude that there is no explicit biblical teaching concerning creation from nothing if the term is understood in the ontological sense that it would later take on. But the seeds of the teaching are found in the biblical texts. It becomes an explicit teaching of the Patristic period as we have seen in the case of the *Shepherd of Hermas* and in the writings of Augustine. And as the concept takes shape in Patristic theology, it comes to be connected with other ideas such as a world of limited, temporal duration.

The concept of creation from nothing arises out of the attempt to shape a clearer understanding of the biblical vision in contrast to the Greek models of world-formation current at that time. It is an attempt to highlight the origin of things in the freedom and creative power of God alone. In its more technical sense the concept will be shaped in later Christian history as an explicitly theological-metaphysical concept of singular importance in giving expression to the Christian understanding of the ultimate origin of the world and of humanity, as we shall see.

II) *Medieval Theology*

This theological development would go on through the centuries, and would reach a high point in the thirteenth-century when Christian scholars engaged the newly discovered thought-world of Aristotle. In the twelfth-century, Anselm made a significant distinction which would become important in later Scholastic theology. He distinguished three possible understandings of the phrase *from nothing*. The first possibility *(necquaquam*

---

[7] *City of God* 11, 6, tr. G. Walsh, D. Zema, G. Monahan, D. Honan (New York: Image, 1960) 211–12.

factum est) would amount to saying *not to be made in any sense.* This would be the case only with God who is not made in any way whatsoever. In this instance to be from nothing simply means not to be made, and it is true only of God. The second possible understanding would involve seeing nothing as some sort of watered-down something. This is clearly inadequate from the perspective of Christian creation-theology since it would mean that that which is said to be from nothing would in fact be from something, however tenuous that something might be.

Only the third meaning is pertinent to the Christian doctrine of creation. Here when something is said to be made from nothing, there is simply nothing pre-existing as material out of which it is made. It is in this sense, argues Anselm, that nothing is to be understood with reference to creation-theology. Here in a truly metaphysical sense of the term, *to be made from nothing* means *to be made, but not from something,* or to come into being from *non-being* in the strict sense of the word. To be created from nothing in this sense would mean to have existence from non-existence.[8] This sort of distinction would be important in the later development of thirteenth century theology.

Matthew of Aquasparta, in the thirteenth century, would appeal to the writings of Averroës to point out that the origin of things could be understood by the philosophical tradition in a variety of ways. Some have seen it as a process through which hidden forms are laid bare for all to see. Others have seen it as a process of separating dissimilar elements from one another. Or one could think of it as a way of bestowing form on matter with a Platonic Demiurge involved in the process. Aristotle envisioned an eternal world in which particular beings emerge from the potency of pre-existent matter to actual existence through the union of matter and form.

Against that background, Christian theology would not accept any theory of eternally existing matter. Nor would it accept any form of emanationism in which created reality is ultimately made of a weakened form of the divine substance. But "nothing comes from nothing." And there is something that exists. If it is not an always existing reality, nor a divine reality, how does it come to be?

The Christian theological answer to that question is to appeal to the creative love of a God who calls things into being from non-being. The nothing of which theology here speaks is not some watered-down form of something. As Anselm had argued, creation from nothing means not an organization of previously unorganized matter. It means simply a being made, but not from something pre-existing. Nothing, therefore, is simply

---

[8] Anselm, *Monologion,* in: *Opera Omnia,* vol. 1, ed. F.S. Schmitt (Edinburgh: Nelson, 1946) 62–66.

non-existence in the most absolute sense of the word. For the great Scholastics like Aquinas and Bonaventure and their contemporaries, creation is not be understood as a physical change. If we can use the word change at all, it must be understood at the metaphysical level to refer to the fact of existence from non-existence. This is not to be understood in a temporal sense, but in a metaphysical sense. There is no subject that passes from non-being to being. Scholastic theology would become even more specific in its language to say that creation is *ex nihilo sui et subjecti*. The word *sui* refers to the particular created being under consideration. The word *subjecti* refers to any material substrate whatever. Neither the created being itself, nor any part of it, pre-exists the divine act of creation.

There is simply the fact of being from non-being. And this is not something that happens by chance. It is something that happens by reason of the intelligent, loving nature of God who calls things into being. To speak of creation from nothing, therefore, is to underscore the sense of absolute dependence on the loving creativity of God who is the ultimate ground of all that exists other than God. The mere fact of created existence is pure gift.

Since this is the case, medieval theology is convinced that, while the world is fundamentally contingent in the sense that it does not have to be at all, it does in fact exist. And it is in fact an orderly world that reflects something of the mind of God. But to say that the world is intelligible is not the same as saying that there cannot be some contingence and random activity within the history of the world. To take intelligibility to mean absolute necessity is to make the created cosmos equivalent to God. Hence Aquinas could argue that it would be contrary to the nature of the created world if nothing ever happened by chance.

In Scholastic language the created world is both true and good. It is known and loved into existence by an intelligent and loving God. This being the case, it is a world that can come to be known and understood, at least to a degree, by intelligent creatures in the world. And it is a world that is worthy of human respect and love as well.

We have already indicated in our discussion of the Scriptures that God creates for a purpose. If now we ask why God creates, we can turn to some of the medieval theologians to see how that question was answered. If we ask Bonaventure, he will answer that God does not create out of any internal divine need to have a world. Nor does anything outside God serve as the motivation for the act of creation. Briefly, it is the nature of the good to pour itself out. The first level at which the divine love pours itself out is internal to the divinity; it is the very life of the trinity itself as an ongoing communion of love. The second level at which the divine love pours itself out is in the act of creating a world external to God. Here Bonaventure says that God creates so as to manifest something of the divine outside the divine life.

We might think of this as analogous to the work of a human artist. Regardless of what internal motivation the artist might have had in producing a work of art, the work itself will stand outside that artist and speak to all who experience it about the person of the artist. So it is that, regardless of any motivation God may or may not have had, the mere fact of the created cosmos will speak about God to those who are capable of beholding it and reflecting on it. The world that comes forth from the creative love of God will manifest something of the richness and glory of the divine externally. And second, since it is the nature of love to share itself, God creates so that creation itself can come to participate in the mysterious fullness and goodness of the divine life of love.

In a similar way Aquinas tells us that God creates because it is the nature of the good to communicate itself. "God intends only to communicate the divine completeness, which is God's goodness. Each and every creature stretches out to its own completion, which is a resemblance of the divine fullness and excellence."[9] The goal which God has in mind in creating, then, becomes the content of the doctrines of salvation, grace, and finally of eschatology. The gift of being that flows from God as creator is laden with the promise of yet fuller, richer being in the future.[10]

In the light of contemporary scientific cosmology, we might wish to ask: Why has God created a world of such baffling immensity and diversity? Though their sense of the cosmos was smaller, the same sort of question was asked by the great medieval theologians. Both Bonaventure and Aquinas appeal to the metaphor of an artist of immensely rich resources. So rich is the divine creative source that no one creature is capable of reflecting it fully. Therefore, it is appropriate that there should be an incredible diversity of creatures, each reflecting something particular about the mystery of the divine. And even more significant is the depth of interrelationships between these diverse creatures. Bonaventure writes:

> There is a multiplicity of beings coming from a single principle because, in fact, there is a first principle, and that first principle is one. Because that principle is simply first, it is fruitful and powerful with a fertility that is immense and infinite. . . . That which is simply first is, for that reason, totally immense. Because of its immensity, it is infinite. And because of the manifestation of its immensity, it shows many of its treasures, but

[9] *Sth.* 1, 44, 4, resp.
[10] For an extended treatment of creation from the perspective of promise, cfr. John F. Haught, *God after Darwin: A Theology of Evolution.* Haught's treatment draws extensively on the implication of the Scriptural background for a theology of promise and relates it explicitly to the understanding of a contemporary scientific cosmology.

not all of them, since the effect cannot be equal to the power of the first cause. . . . Because of its supreme power, it can produce many things. Because of its supreme wisdom, it knows many things. And because of its supreme goodness, it wishes to communicate itself to many things and to produce many things. Therefore, a multiplicity of things emerges from one principle precisely because the principle is first and single.[11]

To the same point, Aquinas writes:

> For God brought things into existence so that God's goodness might be communicated to creatures, and be represented through them. And because one single creature was not enough, God produced many and diverse things so that what was wanting in one expression of the divine goodness might be supplied by another; for goodness, which in God is single and uniform, in creatures is multiple and divided. Hence, the whole universe less incompletely than one creature alone shares and represents God's goodness.[12]

The cosmos is not just a profusion of isolated beings that, in their individuality, speak of God. In its totality, it speaks of the same God. We will discuss this more fully in the next chapter which deals with the mystery of the Trinity.

III) *Continuous Creation*

It was common in the theological tradition to speak not only of creation from nothing, but to speak also of God's ongoing sustaining activity. The conviction that stood behind this was the understanding that if God were to withdraw the divine activity, the creature would lapse back to the nothingness from which it had come. As Augustine expresses it: ". . . creatures would cease to exist altogether if the motion of divine Wisdom disposing all graciously, were withdrawn from them."[13]

And Aquinas writes:

> The conservation of things by God does not take place by reason of a new action, but by means of the continuation of that action by which God confers being. This is an action subject to neither time nor to change. An example would be the light that is maintained in the atmosphere by the sun's continuous shining.[14]

[11] *II Sent.* d.1, p.2, a.1, q.1 (II, 40).
[12] *Sth.* 1, 47, 1, resp.
[13] *The Literal Meaning of Genesis* 4, 12.
[14] *Sth.* 1, 104, 1, ad 4.

If creation involves the initial conferral of being, conservation is the continued conferral of being. This was commonly understood to be related to God's omnipresence, to divine providence, and to the divine governance of the world.

As the primal source of being in creation, God is internally present to all things as long as they exist.[15] Peter Lombard formulated the doctrine of divine presence in a way that would become common in medieval theology. "God is in everything by essence, by power, and by presence; and in the saints by grace; and in the man Christ by reason of union."[16] From this, medieval theologians would commonly speak of an essential presence, a dynamic presence, and a presence by virtue of knowledge.

As sources for this teaching, Lombard appeals to Gregory the Great, Augustine, Hilary, and Ambrose. Thus, while the doctrine of creation from nothing highlights the idea of divine transcendence, the doctrine of divine presence emphasizes the sense of divine immanence. The polarity between these is basic to a proper understanding of the relation of creation to the Creator. God is God, and not the world. The world is the world, and not God. But the world is and remains only because of the ongoing presence of the divine creative activity. As Aquinas puts it: "God operates within things as the first agent, but not in a way that makes the activity of the created causes superfluous."[17]

There is nothing that stands in the way of an effect issuing from both a primary cause and a secondary cause, provided that each operates at the level proper to its nature. God's causality does not replace secondary causality but makes the latter possible. Secondary causality is genuinely real. When we think of this in terms of the classical world-view marked by stability, our tendency is to see the continuous creative action of God as the sustaining power that does not allow things to lapse into nothingness and that allows the potentiality of fixed natures to come to fruition.

In Scholastic theology the term *providence* is understood to refer to the conviction that there is an eternal, divine plan for creation and its history. Scripture in both Testaments gives eloquent expression to the sense of divine providence. In the Hebrew Scriptures this is particularly the case in the reflection on the vagaries of Israelite history. The prophetic reflection never lost the sense of God's abiding presence and care for the people. In the teaching of Jesus we read:

> Look at the birds of the sky. They do not sow or reap, they gather nothing into barns; yet your heavenly Father feeds them. Are you not more im-

[15] *Sth.* 1, 8, 1.
[16] *Sententiae* I, d. 37, 1, 2.
[17] *Sth.* 1, 105, 5.

portant than they. . . . Why are you anxious about clothes? Learn from the way the wild flowers grow. They do not work or spin. But I tell you that not even Solomon in all his splendor was clothed like one of these. If God so clothes the grass of the field which grows today and is thrown into the oven tomorrow, will he not much more provide for you? (Matt 6:26-30).

In more technical language of theology the sense of divine providence can be described as: "The ordering of creatures to an end that pre-exists in the mind of God."[18] Seen in this way, it corresponds with the theological conviction that God has both an intellect and a will. God knows and wills things into existence. Hence, one expects creation to reflect something of the divine intelligibility in itself.

The working out of the divine plan in time is designated with the word *governance*. Vatican Council I, in response to what it felt to be movements of fatalism, materialism, and mechanism, formulated its understanding of the issue in the following terms:

> All things that have been created God protects and governs by means of divine providence that "reaches from end to end mightily, and governs all things well" (Wis 8:1). For all things are bare and open to God's eyes (Heb 4:13) even those things which are yet to be by the free action of creatures.[19]

At one level these ideas give expression to the theological conviction concerning the abiding presence and action of God in relation to creation and history. This is an important issue that points away from the impersonal and at times fatalistic understanding of the cosmos that appears in the writings of some cosmologists. But all the above is formulated against the background of the physical world-view that has lost its power for our contemporary scientific culture.

IV) *Some Contemporary Theological Insights*

The question today, then, is how to envision this ongoing creative action of the divine in relation to a cosmos not of fixed natures, but to a cosmos that is incomplete and still unfolding. Here, as we might expect, there is no final and satisfactory answer to the question.

A helpful approach may be found in the work of Process theology inspired by the philosophy of A. N. Whitehead. The Whiteadean vision of

---

[18] *Sth.* 1, 22, 1.
[19] *Denzinger/Schönmetzer, Enchiridion Symbolorum* ed. 32 (Herder, 1963) 3003. Will be cited as "DS."

reality sees the cosmos as essentially open-ended and incomplete. All is taken up in a process of becoming what it has not yet been. In relation to creation, God is seen as the source of all possibilities. If we envision these possibilities to be calling creatures from their present to a future, we can think of God, the source of these possibilities, as a magnetic power from the future drawing out the possibilities of what is there. The view of White-head is shaped largely by philosophical insights. To what degree it may be connected with Scripture can be debated.

Reflecting a similar orientation, but providing a more explicitly biblical orientation is the work of Moltmann. He sees the traditional understanding of continuous creation to mean basically the continuous sustaining of the creation brought into being at the beginning. In this sense God does not create anything new, but continually creates what was once created in the beginning. This is fine as far as it goes, argues Moltmann. But if we look at the Scriptures, we find not only the language about creation, but language about the new creation. This is not only the preservation of the original creation, but a creative activity of God which innovates. "God's historical activity is then eschatologically oriented: it preserves the initial creation by anticipating the consummation and by preparing the way for that consummation. The historical activity of God has cosmic dimensions; it brings the whole cosmos into a new condition."[20]

Drawing directly from the biblical tradition, Moltmann contrasts the effortless creativity of God as described in Genesis with the burdensome character of God's creativity in history where the Creator has to deal with the problems brought about through the creatures which the Creator has made.

> The creation of salvation proceeds out of the suffering of contradiction. The creation of righteousness proceeds out of the suffering of injustice. So God's creations in history contain at once passion and action. Even the traditional doctrine which teaches that God sustains the world in spite of its sin, already saw this as God's patience, and understood it as an expression of God's long-suffering. The inexhaustible creative power of God in history always makes itself known first of all in the inexhaustibility of the power of God's suffering. This is not a sign of God's weakness; it is the revelation of God's strength.[21]

In this sense Moltmann moves from biblical material in a direction which has some of the overtones of Whitehead who argued against the tendency of classical Christianity to turn God into an oriental potentate when the

---

[20] J. Moltmann, *God in Creation: A New Theology of Creation and the Spirit of God* (Minneapolis: Fortress, 1993) 210.
[21] *Ibid.*

most important clues of the Christian Scriptures point to the importance of the tender, evocative love of God as the truly creative power that undergirds reality.[22]

Polkinghorne offers some reflections that are more directly reflective of the sciences. God allows creation to shape itself "through the shuffling explorations of contingency." Polkinghorne speaks of God as the source and guide of the fruitfulness of a universe which is marked by a sense of deep order and remarkable fruitfulness. The idea of continuous creation is a way of conceptualizing the ongoing relation of God to the cosmos which highlights the sense of divine immanence.[23]

The most thorough and consistent development in this direction is found in Haught's book *God after Darwin*.[24] Moving from the scriptural theology of promise, Haught develops the implications of promise through philosophical insights drawn from Whitehead, Hans Jonas, and Michael Polanyi. His discussion leads to a fundamental restructuring of the theological landscape.

V) *Scientific Theories of Origins*

From this perspective it is interesting to look at the work of contemporary scientific cosmologists and authors who discuss the work of the sciences. When contemporary scientists use the language of nothingness, they raise the expectation that they intend to speak about an issue which, when viewed against the background of the tradition of Western philosophy and theology, moves beyond the limits of scientific methodology. The fact that they do this may be taken as a symptom of the limits of scientific methodology and of the tendency of the human mind to move further beyond what is fair game for science as an empirically grounded enterprise.

It is important to say clearly that the nothing spoken of by contemporary scientists, especially in the context of quantum-wave fluctuation mentioned above, is not the nothing spoken of by traditional Christian theology as we have just described it. In classical philosophical thought, no accident exists without inhering in a substance. The wave spoken of in quantum explanations of the origin of the universe looks ominously like what classical thought envisioned as an accident. This means that it is inconceivable that there would be a wave without having something that is waving. When one speaks of a quantum wave, therefore, there must be something to wave. It may be that this is not at all like what we ordinarily experience, but it is

---

[22] A. N. Whitehead, *Adventures of Ideas* (New York: Free Press, 1933, 1961) 166–67.

[23] John Polkinghorne, *Science and Theology: An Introduction* (London and Minneapolis: SPCK and Fortress, 1998) 80–81.

[24] Haught, *God after Darwin: A Theology of Evolution*.

something in some form. The medieval idea of nothing, on the other hand, is simply and totally the denial of existence in any form whatsoever.

The tendency of physicists to move in this direction, then, raises the question about the nature of science and the limit experiences to which science itself gives rise. What does one say when one is pushed against such outer limits? Is this a question of saying that, if science can neither ask the question nor provide an answer if the question is asked, then we have a meaningless question? To assume that is to take a position of pure scientific positivism. Philosophically such a position can be shown to be self-contradictory, since the scientific enterprise itself is based on assumptions that cannot be empirically verified.

Another possibility is to say that we must recognize the limitations placed on science by virtue of its own methodology if we understand it to be a purely empirical discipline, as some fancy it to be. Or we might recognize that scientists themselves are divided between those who are primarily observers (or empirically oriented) and those who are theoreticians (or speculatively oriented). Observations and speculation are clearly two elements or dimensions of contemporary cosmology as we know it. The subtitle of George Gamow's book *One, Two, Three, Infinity* makes the point with remarkable brevity. It reads simply: *Facts and Speculations of Science*. Much of the work of scientists such as Hawking and Tipler would come under the category of speculation rather than that of observation. One hopes that at some point empirical observations will confirm the speculation. But in the first instance, much of it is speculation.

While speaking of scientific methodology, we must recognize that, however we may prefer to envision the methodology of science, there are dimensions to human experience and human questioning that are not accounted for by any positivistic understanding of science. We refer especially to areas such as aesthetic and religious experience. Regardless of how one accounts for these dimensions of our experience, they are real elements of human experience. And questions do arise from these dimensions of experience which are not properly the domain of the positive sciences.

In reading the argument above about the meaning of creation from nothing, it is important to keep in mind precisely what is involved in the so-called Big Bang model of cosmology. Already in the 1920s, A. Friedman had suggested the possibility of a constantly expanding universe. In 1927 G. Lemaitre showed that an expanding universe could be seen as an implication of Einstein's theory of relativity. This could be connected with E. Hubble's study of the red-shift in distant galaxies. The red-shift has to do with the fact that the spectral lines of distant galaxies show a definite shift to the red end of the spectrum. And this red-shift is stronger in the case of more distant galaxies. Why is this? If they are moving away from us, that would provide a possible explanation, since light moving away from the observer shifts to the red end of the spectrum. But how could they be moving away? Perhaps this could be because the whole cosmos is expanding.

So, Gamow could compare our universe to a large balloon being inflated. Like the balloon, our universe is expanding. And with the expansive movement, the galaxies are moving apart from each other like the spots on the skin of a balloon. Hence, some form of an expanding universe seems to suggest itself.

The argument looks roughly like this. If the universe is expanding, what did it look like before? Can we trace it backward in time to its original situation? What would the initial conditions of the cosmos have been like. It seems that space would have been minimal while energy would have been maximal and highly concentrated. The whole would have been perhaps no larger than the size of a pinhead. For some unknown reason, the expansion of that pure, concentrated energy began, and it continues to the present time. Within the first few minutes of this expansion, the process produced what we know today as subatomic particles—protons, neutrons, and electrons. As space continued to expand, things began to cool down and gradually atoms could be formed. Physicists offer many details of the stages of this process. Basically, we are interested in the claim that the process of expansion has continued for some fifteen billion years until it has brought forth the cosmos as we now observe it. But it is not clear whether this expansion will continue indefinitely; or whether at some point things will begin to contract and eventually return to something like its small origins.

Thus the Big Bang model of cosmology is a theoretical construct which helps explain some empirical data. In this case we begin with the observation of the red shift. Given the theory of expansion, the next step for a scientist is to see if any other data will confirm or deny the theory. Hence, the significance of the discovery of the cosmic background radiation by Arno Penzias and Robert Wilson in 1965; for it was seen to provide a significant confirmation of the Big Bang theory. To this we might add the inflationary thesis of Alan Guth in 1975, and the work of G. Smoot and colleagues in 1992. But this is not the end of the story. There was and still are competitive cosmological models. But the Big Bang model seems most convincing to a large number of cosmologists at present.

To the degree that physics is an empirical science, the methodology is by nature inductive. That means, until all the evidence has been discovered and accounted for, a theory has not been definitively proven, at least not in the classical sense of a strict demonstration. To the degree that any large cosmological vision depends on the data of physics, or is confirmed by the data of physics, such a vision is always temporary and open-ended until all the data are in.

Does the Big Bang model describe a fact? As of now we cannot say. Does the model help understand some significant data? Yes. Might there be conflicting data which might eventually lead to the rejection of the model? Yes. This is just to underline some important aspects involved in the very nature of scientific methodology. Our intention is not to put down the sciences. It is merely to underscore the limitations that are involved in scientific claims of any sort. For the time being, it might be helpful to think of the Big Bang as a suggestive and helpful image or metaphor rather than as a literal description of cosmic facts. And when physicists who represent Big Bang cosmology begin to speak of creation from nothing, either they have moved beyond the limits of their discipline, or they have in mind with these words something quite different from what these words have meant in classical Christian theology.

If "nothing comes from nothing," as the ancient Greeks would have it, how do we explain the fact that there is something that does not have to be? The answer to that for classical Christian theology is not some weakened, watered down type of something, but simply the creative love of God who calls things into being from non-being. For Scholastic thought, this is not a physical change. As we have suggested above, we might be tempted to call it a metaphysical change, provided we recognize that there is no common subject on both sides of the change. There is not something that passes from non-being to being. There is simply the fact of being from non-being. This is a matter not of temporal priority but of ontological priority. It is not a continuation of the chain of secondary causality to one more, and presumably final, link in the chain. It is a move to a fundamentally different level of causality. God is not a cause among causes at the beginning of the temporal chain of created causes. Rather, God is the ground for the fact that there is created causality at all at every moment of time.

In this sense there is no temporal *before* with respect to the moment of creation. The creative activity of God is not limited to the first moment of time. It is always the ground of created causality throughout the entire history of the cosmos. Simply put, *God* is the name for that which exists by virtue of its own nature and has the reason for its existence in itself rather than in another. *Creature* is a name for that whose existence is fundamentally contingent and finite. It does not have the reason for its existence in itself. If it has a reason for existence, then, and that reason is not in the creature itself, it follows that the reason for its existence must be in another.

How, then, does theology understand the existence of the cosmos? From a theological perspective, creation exists only by virtue of a free, loving act of the divine will, not by virtue of any sort of necessity. Since it is grounded in divine freedom, it is essentially contingent; it does not have to be. But since the divine is also intelligent, one expects that the cosmos that comes from that source will also be intelligible. One might want to relate this to the scientific view which says that, while the cosmos seems to be intelligible at some level, yet "it just happens to be."

Big Bang cosmology can be seen as a scientific model that lays out, in the light of current scientific knowledge, what Scholastics had called secondary causality. Quantum physics today may make it troublesome to describe all inner-worldly processes with the language of causality. We can use this language even though we may prefer to think of scientific views as descriptive rather than as causal statements. When the question of the Big Bang model is viewed this way, it cannot raise the question much less suggest an answer to the question as to *why* there is anything to bang at the proposed beginning of time. This might be just the issue that surfaces at the end of S. Hawking's *A Brief History of Time*. When we have given a complete explanation of what the cosmos is and how it works, writes Hawking, then we can ask the really interesting question: Why? A few remarks about this would be in place.

A scientific question about "why" is answered by tracing a given state of affairs to a prior state of affairs. "D" is because of "C," which is because of "B," which is because of "A," etc. An apple is there, because there is a tree, which is there because a seed fell to the ground and was germinated, etc. When you have given an account of all secondary causality, which we may take to be the complete explanation of what the cosmos is and how it operates of which Hawking speaks—which is presumably the point of the search for a Theory of Everything or a Grand Unified Theory that produced so many books on the market a few years ago—then you arrive at the question which is no longer approachable by scientific methodology. Why is there anything to operate this way at all? If this is a question about inner-worldly causality—which is the fair domain of science—then the prior assumption that we have given a complete explanation of the cosmos is erroneous. But if this is not just another question of inner-worldly causality, then what is it? It seems clear that it is no longer a scientific question. Whether it is a meaningful question will depend on what your basic philosophy of life and of science might be. Yet it is precisely this question to which theology addresses itself in the form of creation-theology.

Another question emerges from contemporary scientific cosmology; this is the question of the time-framework involved. Classical Western thought had considered the age of the universe to be a few thousand years. Today, one of the common projections among scientists is 15 billion years, plus or minus a few billion years depending on how one determines the Hubble constant. Numbers like this can be written or said; they can hardly be imagined. Does the idea of such a history fly in the face of Christian faith?

When modern cosmologists speak of the age of the cosmos, they are speaking the language of time. If we understand this issue from the perspective of Scholastic theology, there is no normative understanding of the length of time involved. Obviously, no theologians of that period would have had any reason to suspect the sort of cosmic age being suggested today. But there is no necessary conflict between the theological idea of a created cosmos and the scientific conjectures of the age of the cosmos. Are we living in a young cosmos, or in an ancient cosmos? Theology itself has no resources for answering that question. If an answer is to be given, it will have to come from the sciences.

From here we can readily ask about the possibility that one might hold the strict theological concept of creation from nothing, which is not a temporal concept, and relate it to the idea of a universe unfolding in time (as is the case with the Big Bang model) rather than to the vision of a universe that comes forth in the first instant of time in a more or less finished form. There is no necessary conflict between the strictly theological, metaphysical notion of creation from nothing, and any particular physical description of the cosmos. The *how* of secondary causality is not the question at this point.

A universe resulting from the fluctuation of a primal vacuum, as suggested by Edward Tryon and others, is not a self-creating universe in the categories of Scholastic theology. Nor is the primal vacuum involved in this physical theory to be identified with the nothingness affirmed by the doctrine of creation out of nothing. Nor is the *nothing* so often referred to by contemporary scientists in any way equivalent to the *nothing* of classical, scholastic theology.

We might conclude that we can be very serious about the theological concept of creation from nothing and have no difficulty accepting Big Bang cosmology as a possible account of the physics of the cosmos. In principle, there need be no contradiction between creation from nothing understood theologically and any particular attempt of science to describe what the cosmos is like and how it works at the physical level.

Theologians by virtue of their discipline have no privileged knowledge of the physics of reality and, like all other people, depend on their own empirical experience and on the work of the sciences for whatever cognitive claims might be made at that level. Scientists, on the other hand, by virtue of their discipline cannot deal with the question of ultimate origin, though they may ask about it as human beings. Obviously conflicts can arise when representatives of either of the disciplines move beyond the limits of their discipline. At that level, however, we are not dealing with a conflict between Christian faith and science. We are confronted rather with a conflict between personal philosophies or world-views.

VI) *Conclusion*

What, then, is expressed in the Christian vision of creation from nothing? Above all, this notion underscores the immediate relation between creation and the Creator. To be created is to exist in absolute dependence on the free, loving creativity of God. Created existence, therefore, in the deepest sense is a pure gift. Beyond this, the concept of creation attempts to express the theological conviction that the created world is to some degree intelligible, though we may have to struggle to come to a deeper understanding of it. It expresses also the conviction that created reality, while radically contingent, does in fact exist for a reason. The creative act of God is not only an act of intelligence, but an act of a purposive will as well. In summary form, to be created means to be from God's orderly love, and to be directed back to that creative, orderly love as to our final goal.

Viewed in this way, creation-theology is a radical denial of any vision of ultimate irrationality and pointlessness. It maintains that, even in the face of great ignorance concerning what the natural world might be and how it operates, we still can live with a sense of confidence that ultimately our existence is meaningful. If the principle of unity and order lies in the will of God, that principle has become manifest to us to some degree in the cosmos itself. It remains for a later chapter to discuss this in relation to christology.

Creation-theology is, further, an attempt to say that it is not only a part of us but rather all that makes us to be human that is from and for God. This means not only our soul, but our bodily reality as well. Thus, Christian confidence in the ultimate meaningfulness of material reality finds its remote ground in the doctrine of creation. As we shall see later, it finds its proximate ground in the Christian belief concerning Christ.

5

The Triune God, the Creator

I) *Augustine and Aquinas*

From Augustine onwards, the works of God *ad extra* were understood to be from God as from one principle. This is maintained even when it is recognized that the one God of whom theology speaks is a triune God. Several times Augustine refers to the mystery of the Son, or the Word, or Wisdom, as emanating from the substance of God and hence as basically different from anything created from nothing. A significant expression of Augustine's position is found in his unfinished book on the Manichees:

> We must explain the Catholic faith first. . . . That faith is the following: God the almighty Father made and established all of creation through the only-begotten Son; that is, through the Wisdom and Power that is consubstantial and coeternal with the Father, in the unity of the Holy Spirit, who is also consubstantial and coeternal. Therefore, the Catholic faith commands that we believe that this trinity is called one God, and that this God has made and created all things that are insofar as they are. So, all of creation, whether spiritual or corporal . . . has been made by God not out of the nature of God, but out of nothing. So it is that nothing of the trinity is to be found in all of creation except the fact that the trinity created it and that it was created. Therefore, we cannot say or believe that the whole of creation is either consubstantial with or coeternal with God.[1]

---

[1] *De Genesi ad litteram, imperfectus liber,* 1, 2.

This may be understood more readily if it is viewed against the background of Augustine's trinitarian speculation. In his work *On the Trinity* Augustine goes to great lengths to develop metaphors for the mystery of the Trinity by turning to the world of human consciousness and interiority. It is there that we encounter the triads: mind—knowledge—love; and memory—intelligence—will. These were to play a major role in subsequent Western Christian theology. As created spirit in human beings involves a movement from simple existence to knowledge and to love. So we may think of the life of the supreme spiritual Being as Being that is the purest knowledge and love.

For Augustine, the expression of God's all-embracing knowledge is the immanent, divine Word. In this Word, also known as the Son, God expresses all that will be created. Everything is created through the Word or the Son in the sense that God has the plan for all of creation in this immanent Word. As the Father and the Son are one principle of the Holy Spirit, so they are, together with the Spirit, one principle of creation. Thus, the divine act of knowledge contains the whole of creation; and the divine act of love embraces all of creation. From this it may be concluded that the free act of creation, as an act of God *ad extra,* is a reflection of the necessary, inner-trinitarian processions of the divine persons.

Given this trinitarian base, Augustine then employs the Platonic tradition of exemplarity to argue that the work of the divine Artist reflects something of the Artist in itself. There is some degree of divine likeness in all of creation. The most remote level of likeness can be called a vestige, or a distant footprint. Beyond that, there is a greater similarity between the Creator and the creature in the case of creatures such as humanity which possess the spiritual powers of intelligence and will. Such a likeness can be called an image of God. So it is that for Augustine, the whole of creation can be seen to be a *carmen Dei* reflecting the mystery of the triune Creator at various levels.

The core of Augustine's position is systematized in the work of Aquinas. In the section of the *Summa* that deals directly with creation, the idea that all the works *ad extra* are from God as one is repeated. As seen by Aquinas, the divine exemplarity is primarily a question of understanding how the Ideas are present in the divine mind. In this sense, "God is the original exemplar of all creatures."[2] Question 44, which consists of four articles, is a strong monadic, monotheistic statement of the nature of the first cause emphasizing the oneness of the creative God. But in Question 45, article 6, the issue of the Trinity appears expressly in the following way. "Hence creation is God's action by reason of God's existence, which is God's very na-

---

[2] *Sth* 1, 44, 3, resp.

ture, and this is common to the three persons. So that creative action is not peculiar to any one person, but is common to the entire Trinity." Aquinas relates this to the Augustinian tradition about God as knowing and willing. God is the cause of things through the divine mind and will, as an artist is related to works of art.

> An artist works through an idea conceived in his mind and through love in his will which is aimed at something. In like manner God the Father wrought creation through his Word, the Son, and through his Love, the Holy Ghost. And from this point of view, keeping in mind the essential attributes of knowing and willing, the processions of the divine Persons can be seen as types for the procession of creatures.

Question 45, article 6, ad 2, presents a traditional Augustinian vision of the inner-trinitarian emanations. The creative power is common to all the persons, but it is theirs in accordance with the order of precedence among the persons. The Son has it from the Father, and the Spirit has it from the Father and the Son. "Hence to be creator is attributed to the Father as to one not having power from another. Concerning the Son, we profess that through him all things were made" thus indicating that the Son is a principle from a principle. And concerning the Spirit, who has the power from both, "we profess that the Spirit guides and quickens all things created by the Father through the Son." Thus we see the doctrine of appropriation at work.

Question 45, article 7, discusses the sense in which we can discover the mark of the Trinity in creatures. Here Aquinas synthesizes the view of Augustine. There is a sense in which every creature is at least a vestige, or a distant representation of God. This may be recognized in the terms "number, weight, and measure" (Wis 11, 21). The human being is seen to be an image of God, reflecting the divine spiritual activity in the experience of knowledge and love.

In Question 46, article 3, he mentions that there are some who read "In the beginning" to refer to the Son as exemplary cause by reason of wisdom. But nowhere do we find any discussion of the significance of the incarnation of the Word of God in relation to creation-theology.

> As efficient causality is appropriated to the Father by reason of power, so exemplary causality is appropriated to the Son by reason of wisdom. Therefore, the verse, "In wisdom you have made them all," is understood to mean that God made all things in the beginning, that is in the Son; as St. Paul writes, ". . . for in him (namely, in the Son) were created all things in heaven and on earth."[3]

---

[3] *Sth* 1, 46, 3. resp. The scriptural citations are: Psalm 104, 24 and Colossians 1, 15-16.

II) *Richard of St. Victor and Bonaventure*

We have spoken above of the Augustinian model of trinitarian theology. Already there we see an attempt to give expression to the relation between the mystery of the Trinity and the reality of creation. This relation emerges with even richer significance in another stream of Western theological tradition. This is a tradition that brings together such names as Pseudo-Dionysius, Richard of St. Victor, and Bonaventure. It is a style of trinitarian reflection which chooses not to take its metaphors from the experience of human interiority. Instead it looks to the neo-Platonic understanding of the primal reality as the Supreme Good, and attempts to relate this philosophical tradition to the biblical conviction that "No one is good but God alone" (Luke 18:19) and that this divine goodness exists in the form of the purest love (1 John 4:8). This tradition, therefore, will involve the interaction of the neo-Platonic idea of the Good, and the scriptural idea of the primal love which is so important in the Johannine material.

The philosophical definition of the good claims that it is the nature of the good to pour itself out or to diffuse itself. "Bonum est diffusivum sui." If God is thought to be the Good in this purely philosophical sense, but not in a trinitarian sense, then some form of self-diffusion is necessarily implied in this definition of the nature of the good. Since it is not immanent as in the case of the Trinity, then it must imply some otherness which is external to the divine; and that is creation. In this case, the emanation of creation appears to be a necessary implication of the very nature of the good. Seen in this way, the creation of the world would be necessary and not free. Hence, from the very definition of the good, we are led to the conclusion that some form of creation is necessary, otherwise we are involved in a contradiction in speaking of a mystery of self-diffusion that does not diffuse itself. Thus if God is simply identified with the philosophical mystery of the Good in the philosophical sense, creation seems to be necessary. But this is not in harmony with the biblical and theological tradition. Therefore, we must look at the possibility of defining the nature of the good from the scriptural understanding of love.

If the Good is love, as in Christian (Johannine) understanding, and if love is understood to be relational, then necessity of some self-diffusion is accounted for within the Godhead itself; the divine is what it is necessarily. The necessary self-diffusion is situated in the mystery of emanation that is internal to the Trinity. The emanation that brings forth the Son from the Father is seen to be the necessary emanation. The mutual relation between the Father and the Son is the mystery from which the Spirit emanates as the emanation of purest love. If God is seen to be the supreme Good in these terms, it follows that God can be thought of as the supreme Good, and yet as free to create or not to create. The internal divine emanations are the presupposition for the external emanation which produces creation. But any emanation external to the divinity is free on the part of God.

This allows for a profound sense of the contingence of the world. God does not need the world in order to be God. In the event that God should create a world, it does not have to be this sort of world. Therefore, from this perspective, if we ask why there is a creation, we can answer in the view of Bonaventure: to manifest the divine goodness; and to allow others to participate in the divine life. Or in Scotus' view, God creates so as to have a perfect, created Lover. The divine act of creation, therefore, is grounded in the primal richness of the triune being of God who is free to share with something external to God, but does not need to do so in order "to be the Good." This leads easily to the understanding of the relation between God's creative activity and the mystery of the incarnate Son as the "point" of creation. This we will treat in detail in chapter 8.

III) *World as Symbol of the Divine Trinity*

The sense of divine purpose is commonly expressed in Scholastic theology with the symbol of a circle. This, in turn, is inspired by the tradition of neo-Platonism. In that philosophical tradition, all pours forth from the primal goodness the nature of which is to communicate itself. All of creation, then is marked by that goodness and carries within itself the desire for final union with the goodness from which it has come.[4] That mystery of primal goodness which for philosophy was an impersonal good can be seen in Christian theology to be the mystery of divine, personal love. And if we think of the emanation of creation as a great chain of being, that chain closes back finally on its point of origin. Thus, the symbol of the circle unites the mystery of origin and end. Here we see an understanding reflected in the great *Summa* writings of the Scholastics which begin with the discussion of God as the source of being and end with the treatment of eschatology where creation closes back on its point of origin. This was not lost, even with the impact of Aristotle on theology in the thirteenth century and beyond.

The image of the circle is used by the Scholastics in a variety of ways. The image of the circle which we have just seen above can be thought of in another way if we imagine the circle to be a river. For, as we read in Eccl 1:7, the river returns to its point of origin. This reading of the scriptural text is drawn from the Latin translation in use in the university context of the

---

[4] Cfr. A. Lovejoy, *The Great Chain of Being: A Study of the History of an Idea* (Cambridge, Mass.: Harvard University Press, 1936).

thirteenth century. It envisions the river flowing from the immensity of the sea and eventually returning to the fullness of its point of origin. The divine Trinity, then, can be seen as the fountain-fullness from which the river of reality flows, both within the mystery of God in the triune life of love, and outside the divinity in the form of creation. The river, then, is a particular way of envisioning the neo-Platonic circle of expansive goodness.[5]

The trinitarian God of productive, creative love can be compared to a living fountain of water. Flowing from that fountain as something known, loved, and willed into being by the creative love of God is the immense river of creation. The world of nature in its vastness is the expression of a loving, intelligent creator. As a reflection of the richness of the creative source, the cosmos can hardly be one-dimensional. On the contrary, like water, it has many dimensions. If, for example, we think of water in the form of a river, it reflects the movement and fluidity of creation. If, on the other hand, we think of water in the form of an ocean, it suggests the over-whelming fullness of creation as it flows from the depths of God. Like an ocean, the cosmos is deep and contains many levels of meaning.

Thus for medieval authors such as Bonaventure, the metaphors of the circle, the river, and water elicit a sense of the immense diversity, fertility, and fluidity of creation. No one form of created being is an adequate expression of the immensely fertile source that resides in the divine, creative love. Therefore, the diversity of beings which in fact exist in creation constitute an appropriate form of divine self-expression. And, as the river eventually closes back on its point of origin, so creation is a dynamic reality, directed in its inner mystery to a fulfillment and completion with God that is the mysterious fruit of its history.

IV) *Contemporary Cosmology as Revelatory*

The world of medieval theology could speak in this way because, for the most part, it viewed the created universe in terms of the Platonic theory of exemplarity. Few of our contemporaries are inclined to think of creation in those terms. But is it possible for us to look at our kind of world and to say in the words of Bonaventure: "Whoever does not see is blind . . . whoever does not hear is deaf . . . whoever does not praise God in all these effects is mute . . . the entire universe will rise up against such a person."[6] Or in the words of Thoreau, "The morning wind forever blows, the poem of creation is uninterrupted; but few are the ears that hear it."[7]

---

[5] Bonaventure, I *Sentences*, prooemium (I, 1ff).
[6] Bonaventure, *Itinerarium* 1, 15 (V, 299).
[7] Henry David Thoreau, *Walden* (New York: Time Inc., 1962) 83.

There are those who maintain that scientific insights into the what and the how of the cosmos tell us nothing about God. For example, T. Ferris asks, from a scientific perspective, what cosmology can tell us about God. "Sadly, but in all earnestness, I must report that the answer as I see it is: Nothing. Cosmology presents us neither the face of God, nor the handwriting of God, nor such thoughts as may occupy the mind of God."[8] His discussion of the issue then seems to focus on attempts to prove the existence of God, or to show from the insights of the sciences that God must have created the universe. And he warns—rightly—against the tendency to fuse the disciplines of science and theology.

Whatever one may think about the argument from design, the cosmological argument, and the ontological proof for the existence of God, it is my view that proving the existence of God in such ways is not the real issue. Of greater importance is to show to what extent a religious faith may be seen not as childish immaturity, but as a responsible vision of the meaning of reality and of human life, and then to search out the possible coherence between the insights of science and those of theology.

It may well be that science, precisely as science and by virtue of scientific methodology, knows nothing about God. This is not a problem as long as we do not claim that science alone defines the range of meaningful discourse. There are clearly other dimensions involved in the human relation to the cosmos. It is our conviction that the entire range of human experiences and questions ought to be brought to bear on our attempts to understand who we are and what sort of world we live in. Science provides important and helpful insights into the physical structure and workings of the cosmos, and it raises important questions that must be addressed by the theologian. The arts, philosophy, and religion open us to other levels of concern about values and meaning, and hence to other levels of questioning.

Religion does not need to appeal either to the sciences or to philosophy to provide its starting point. This might have been the understanding of an older form of apologetic. But what is of interest to a reflective religious believer at the present time is the question as to whether we may see a certain sort of coherence between the concerns of religion and the insights of science. Is it possible to ask whether a person who believes in the Christian God can look out at the physical cosmos with the lense of contemporary science instead of with the lense of an archaic medieval physics? If the believer does this, what does such a person see in the cosmos? How can the cosmos, viewed in the light of the best empirical knowledge available to us through the sciences, be said to manifest the mystery of God to those who

---

[8] Timothy Ferris, *The Whole Shebang: A State of the Universe(s) Report* (New York: Simon and Schuster, 1997) 303–4.

believe in God, and who believe that the physical universe which is described by the sciences is the universe which God is creating?

Clearly we do not find the geocentric cosmos of the pre-modern world. Nor do we find the mechanistic and utterly predictable cosmos of Newtonian thought. But we find a cosmos which evokes a profound sense of its seemingly impenetrable mystery. Apparently boundless in space and time, or at least beyond our power to imagine, it is a dynamic, unfolding, organically inter-related cosmos, marked by some degree of unpredictability together with forms of order which are at times unexpected and yet remarkable in their beauty.

The conviction of pre-modern Christianity was that if one learns to read the book of the cosmos correctly, one will discover something of God's wisdom, beauty, power, and love. To see the cosmos as a theophany means to see the various forms and rhythms of nature as at least distant reflections of divine qualities. Is that possible for us today? If we think of the cosmos as a book, then we might ask what are the words in the book? If we think of the words as part of a song, we might ask what does the song sound like when we hear the whole?

The cosmos as we now see it reveals a baffling number of diverse forms of created beings. This has been the focus of E.O. Wilson's extensive work over many years on the diversity of life. We might think also of S.J. Gould's work.[9] At one level Gould describes the apparently haphazard character of the process commonly called evolution. At another level, he argues about the variety of life forms within the full house of our planet's history. Without discussing Gould's argument against the idea that evolution is a movement toward more excellent and more complex forms of life that finds its summit in humankind, what is interesting here is the other side of the argument; namely, that there is one discernible trend in evolution, and that is the emergence of an ever greater variety of organisms. Hence the title: *Full House*. Thus, from a scientific perspective, the emergence of such prolific diversity is a fact that cries out for some sort of interpretation. While Gould has his own form of interpretation, faith and theology can see the same diversity as an expression of the divine fecundity of being poured out in such richness that it would not be appropriately expressed in a single form or even in a few forms of created being.

While the understanding of the physics of the universe in the medieval period, limited though it was, could evoke a sense of the richness of the divinity, it seems that the contemporary vision can do so even more emphatically. Who can look at and study the teeming life-forms of this planet and

---

[9] Stephen Jay Gould, *Full House: The Spread of Excellence from Plato to Darwin* (New York: Harmony Books, 1996).

not ask: What has God done? What sort of God has done this? Perhaps the metaphor of the ocean might be appropriate to evoke the sense of the fullness of being reflected in the cosmos. What might this suggest concerning a proper respect for even the smallest of creatures and their place in the cycles of life?

Scientists today are inclined to see a universe of things intimately intertwined at all levels. Think, for example, of the search for the ultimate particle. By and large, it has been assumed that the subatomic particles are isolated and independent particles. Yet in the quark research being done at Fermilab near Chicago it seems that quarks are discerned only in groups. If quarks are really the end of the line in the search for the ultimate building blocks, this may mean that the so-called building blocks are not isolated monadic blocks, but are relational complexes. This points to the possibility that the cosmos is really systems within systems all the way down, and all the way out. If this is the case, then it seems that created reality is through and through relational.

With that in mind, we can recall the core insight of the traditional trinitarian concept of God; namely, that the divine reality is intrinsically relational in character. It may well be, then, that Christian believers today can see the cosmos as grounded in and as reflecting the relational character of the Trinity. Similarly, if the Trinity is thought of, as it is in the tradition, as a unity of many, it may be thought of as reflected in the cosmic system of systems; a union of many and not simply a universe of individual things only extrinsically related to each other.

These are some of the ways in which nature can still be seen as a revelation of God. It is through nature that God brings us into being and sustains us. To know nature more deeply is to sense its mystery, its depth, and its value. It is to know nature as a reflection of the sacred; a sacrament of the divine. The cosmos truly speaks to us of God. But what it says is difficult to discern. Yet, in all this, we see "indistinctly, as in a mirror" (1 Cor 13:12).

6

Humanity in the Cosmic Context

I) *Problem of Anthropocentrism*

Western culture has lived for many centuries with the conviction that humanity stood at the center of the created order, and that all other things were there for humans to use for their own ends. We have already described the Aristotelian-Ptolemaic cosmology in which much of medieval understanding was shaped. In a very literal, physical sense, earth was the center of the universe with the other planets and stars surrounding it in a series of concentric circles. The earth was literally the center of things. On the earth, humanity, with its intellect and will, was the center of things on planet earth. It is possible to find texts in Scripture that seem to harmonize with this view, and which could be easily taken as a religious legitimation for what otherwise might seem to be merely a secular vision of reality.

But even with this anthropocentric sense in medieval times, there was still a sense of the way in which humanity was interwoven with the physical world. The macrocosm, or the great world, was compacted in the microcosm, or humanity. That is, all the elements that made up the world at large are contained in a concentrated way in human nature. Christian theology, therefore, could see all of creation serving humanity in as far as the mysteries of nature awaken the human spirit to give praise to God the Creator. This is a long way from the understanding of more recent generations. If anthropocentrism was a fact, in medieval times it was not the same as the anthropocentrism of modern times.

But a lethal wound was delivered to this sense of humanity when the Copernican revolution took the earth out of the physical center, and placed it in an orbit circling the sun together with the other planets. Humanity's physical home was no longer the center of the universe. What does that mean concerning humanity itself? As if that were not bad enough, the evolutionary vision of the nineteenth century that will be discussed below traced humanity itself back to some pre-human form of animal life. Add to this the contours of contemporary cosmology with its sense of the immensity of both space and time in this universe which really seems to have no center, and the context for human self-understanding is changed dramatically.

Coming at the question of anthropocentrism from yet another perspective, the sense of environmental problems in recent decades has given rise to a number of very sharp critiques of the biblical tradition. These critiques have made the claim that the real source of the environmental problems as we know them at present is to be found precisely in the biblical tradition.

II) *The Biblical Tradition*

A) *Recovery of the Biblical Tradition*

Much of the problem of human self-understanding that stands behind the technological culture of the modern Western world has been attributed to the biblical tradition, and more specifically to the text of Genesis:

> Then God said: "Let us make man in our image, after our likeness. Let them have dominion over the fish of the sea, the birds of the air, and the cattle, and over all the wild animals and all the creatures that crawl on the ground."
> God created man in his image; in the divine image he created him; male and female he created them. God blessed them, saying: "Be fertile and multiply; fill the earth and subdue it. Have dominion over the fish of the sea, the birds of the air, and all the living things that move on the earth" (Gen 1:26-28).

Two issues stand out: the metaphor of image and the commission to fill the earth and subdue it. It is not difficult to see that at times this could be interpreted as a command to exploit the resources of the earth on behalf of humanity. Taken together, these two ideas seem to lend themselves to a strongly anthropocentric understanding. When this is brought together with an Enlightenment understanding of humanity and connected with the possibilities opened up by modern technology, it can easily become the recipe for wanton destruction of many of God's creatures.

If it has happened in the past that the text was interpreted in this way, modern exegesis has changed the situation significantly. At one level, the metaphor of image of God must be read in terms of the historical context and the sources used in composing this text. From this perspective, the metaphor of image itself says nothing about ruling or having dominion. It points, rather, to the sense of a particular closeness to God not found in other creatures. It points also to a particular function. For the human being is to be a representative of God in relation to the rest of creation.

At another level, the text of the Priestly account becomes more complex to unravel. The so-called commission seems to describe the relation of humanity to the entire created realm, and the dependence of humanity on the other creatures at least for nourishment. The call "to subdue the earth," when viewed in the original context, refers to the way a people takes possession of what is to be its homeland. Certainly in view of the experience of the Jewish people in antiquity, this did not include the idea of random exploitation. Twice the text uses the language of dominion to speak of humanity's relation with animals. If the context for this is the Jewish theology of kingship, it would be a way of saying that humanity, like a good king, is responsible for the good of the entire realm. The king is one who mediates blessings to the realm. Or if one thinks of the text in terms of an agrarian culture, it would seem to refer to the domestication of animals by human beings. After this the text goes on to describe a situation that can best be described as vegetarian.

> See, I have given you every plant yielding seed that is upon the face of the earth and every tree with seed in its fruit. You shall have them for food. And to every beast of the earth, and to every bird of the air, and to everything that creeps on the earth, everything that has breath of life, I have given every green plant for food (Gen 1:29-30).

This could well be related to Genesis 2:15 of the Yahwist account in which God settles the first human in the garden to cultivate and care for it. Here, without using the metaphor of image, the text suggests the idea of a responsible gardener. Taking both of these texts together, it is possible to say that, according to the original intent of the redactor, the role of humanity is to so relate to the other creatures that in these relations, something of the creative love and care of God will become manifest in visible form within the created world. When the text is read in this way, it does not suggest anything like a reckless, domineering subjection of all creatures to humanity, much less a wanton exploiting of creation for human use and enjoyment with no other concern in mind.

B) *Teaching of Vatican II*

Something of this interpretation can be found in the way Vatican Council II makes use of the text:

Throughout the course of the centuries, human beings have labored to improve the circumstances of their lives through a monumental amount of individual and collective effort. To believers, this matter is clear: considered in itself, such human activity accords with God's will. For humanity, created in God's image, received a mandate to subject to itself the earth and all that it contains, and to govern the world with justice and holiness; a mandate to relate humanity itself and the totality of things to God who was to be acknowledged as the Lord and Creator of all. Thus, by the subjection of all things to humanity, the name of God would be made glorious throughout all the earth.[1]

It is important to note how the human governance of the world is qualified in this text. It is to be a governance in which justice and holiness qualify the inner-worldly relations of humanity to all other creatures, and the whole of creation with humanity to God. The text goes on to say that when women and men are living and acting in a way that benefits society:

. . . they can justly think that by their work they are unfolding the work of the Creator, taking into account the well-being of their fellow human beings, and contributing by their personal efforts to the realization of the divine plan in history. . . . Thus, far from thinking that works produced by human talent and energy are in opposition to God's power, and that the rational creature exists as a kind of rival to the Creator, Christians are convinced that the triumphs of the human race are a sign of God's greatness and the fruitfulness of God's own ineffable design.[2]

In this way the Council speaks of the meaning of the biblical text which highlights the distinctiveness of humanity as God's creature. At one level, humanity is profoundly rooted in the material of the created universe. ". . . Humanity is not allowed to despise its bodily life. Rather human beings are obliged to regard the body as good and honorable since God has created it and will raise it up on the last day."[3]

At another level, humanity is distinctive—created in the image of God. But that distinctiveness does not severe our relation to the rest of the created order. Humanity is that point within creation where the mute creation becomes consciously aware of its relation to God and raises its voice in a hymn of praise.

Consisting of a unity of body and soul, human nature, by virtue of its bodily dimension, gathers within itself the elements of the material world. Thus these elements reach their high point through humanity, and through human beings they raise their voice in free praise of the Creator.[4]

[1] *Gaudium et spes,* n. 34.
[2] *Ibid.*
[3] *Op. cit.,* n. 14.
[4] *Ibid.*

This suggests an understanding of humanity and its relation to the created world far different from that of Enlightenment philosophy or that of the contemporary technological culture.

Precisely in terms of the body, human beings are interwoven in the web of the material creation, but because of their intellect "they surpass the material universe, for they share in the light of the divine mind."[5] At this level, they may be seen as creation come to self-awareness and capable of interacting with the world in ways that may be either creative or destructive. How will this be done so as to reflect genuine "justice and sanctity" in the world? Similar to the biblical sense that humanity should come to reflect the loving creativity and care of God within creation, this conciliar text again raises the question of an appropriate ethical response to the distinctive situation of humanity within the whole of creation. Humanity is capable of taking up the chemical process that begets life into its own hands and to change it. In this sense, humanity reflects the creative power of God. But what sort of changes will be truly life-giving and what sort of changes might be destructive?

There can be little doubt that the early biblical texts see humanity commissioned in some way to reflect the creativity of God within the world. What that will mean in a world that has the scientific and technological possibilities of the contemporary world must be an area of very serious ethical reflection. This is perhaps one of the areas where the need for conversation between the knowledge of science and the wisdom of the religious traditions is called for in a dramatic way.

III) *Theological Tradition*

Rooted as humanity is in the earth, there is a sense in which the human being is deeply oriented to God. Early in the Patristic period of Christian history, humanity was seen basically as an openness to God. In the most fundamental sense, the human person is understood to be *capable of the divine.* This relates to the common Patristic understanding of grace as a self-communication of the divine to human beings. A common formulation of the early Fathers is: God became human so that humans could become God-like. By reason of grace, the human person is called to share in all that God is by nature.

In Scholastic theology we encounter the idea that such a divine self-communication is seen to be possible without destroying human nature as such. Aquinas, for example, was convinced that the human person is naturally inclined to its ultimate end which is God. But it is incapable of attaining

[5] *Op. cit.,* n. 15.

that end except through grace.[6] Can this be seen to be a natural desire for
the supernatural? Some theologians will see it that way. The deepest potential in humanity is the potential for receiving the mystery of divine
grace in the depth of the human person. It is precisely that potency which
lies at the heart of human nature that has been brought to act in the most
sublime way in the mystery of the incarnation. A significant example of
this conviction is found in a Christmas sermon by Bonaventure where we
read:

> The ability of human nature to be united in a unity of person with the di-
> vine—which is the most noble of all the receptive potencies implanted in
> human nature—is reduced to act so that it would not be a mere empty po-
> tency. And since it is reduced to act, the perfection of the entire created
> order is realized, for in that one being the unity of all reality is brought to
> consummation.[7]

At times, especially in the post-Reformation period of Catholic theology, the relation between human nature and grace is seen as a mere lack of
repugnance between them. Grace presupposes nature, and it does not destroy nature. But nature cannot lay claim to grace as a right. To argue that
nature can make such a claim would make the gift-character of grace to be
impossible. The human person, therefore, cannot have a natural desire for
that which is by definition above and beyond human nature. Hence, there
can be no natural desire for the supernatural. This will be reflected in the
Baroque theories of a *pure* nature which has its own, immanent, natural
end.

A concern similar to that of Patristic and Scholastic theology is reflected
in the more recent work of M. Blondel and H. De Lubac, both of whom
tend to speak of a natural desire for the supernatural.

> If there is in our nature the desire to see God, that is possible only be-
> cause God wishes to give us a supernatural end which consists in seeing
> God. . . . That is not to say that the human being, because of this desire,
> demands that it be fulfilled. On the contrary, it is because God wishes to
> give this fulfillment to humanity that the human person is obliged to tend
> to possess it.[8]

The same tendency appears also in the more recent ideas of transcendental anthropology. This is a style of reflection that prefers to emphasize

---

[6] *In Boeth. de Trinitate,* q. 6, a. 4, ad 5.

[7] "Sermon II on the Nativity of the Lord," in: *What Manner of Man?* tr. Zachary Hayes,
O.F.M. (Chicago: Franciscan Herald Press, 1974) 74.

[8] Henri de Lubac, *The Mystery of the Supernatural* (New York: Herder & Herder, 1967)
486, 489.

the concrete world in which human beings actually find themselves, and not any theoretically possible worlds different from this one. Transcendental theology thinks of this world and of humanity in it in terms of God's intent in creating. This means that the actual world in which humans find themselves has never existed independently of God's will to communicate the divine to personal creatures in a personal way. The whole of history in this world is touched by divine grace. Within such a world the human person is constantly drawn beyond itself. It moves in a seemingly endless human reach outward from the hidden inner core of the person to the world of persons and things, and through these beings, to the mystery of the divine. It is in terms of this movement that transcendental thought tends to view the relation of human nature to God. God is, as it were, like a magnet that draws the human spirit through all its contacts with persons and objects in the world around it. The human person, on the other hand, experiences an ongoing movement of self-transcendence which is, at least implicitly, an experience of God.

It is above all this understanding of humanity as deeply oriented to God that runs through the theological tradition in a variety of forms, and that becomes an issue when we begin to think in terms of contemporary evolutionary perspectives.

IV) *Biological Evolution and Catholic Theology*

In terms of its etymology, before any specific, technical meaning is given to it, the word *evolution* simply points to a process of unfolding or development whereby one being realizes its native potential, or one being is derived from another. In terms of the sciences at the present time, the word can be used in its broadest sense to refer to the development of the cosmos as a whole. This refers to the big picture which is commonly described as cosmic evolution. Within our vision of a cosmos which, in its entirety, is still incomplete and unfolding, we distinguish a specific dimension of that unfolding in the movement from pre-life to life, and then to intelligent life. This is commonly named biological evolution.

Within the context of biological evolution it is possible to distinguish between macroevolution and microevolution. The first refers to the process whereby one species arises from another species. The second refers to changes that take place within a species. Beyond this, when the cosmos has brought intelligent life into being, we then discover the history of the ways in which these intelligent creatures have attempted to structure their life together. This is known as cultural or social evolution. All of these belong to the total picture when we speak of evolution from a scientific perspective today. But for our purpose in this chapter, we will limit our discussion to the phenomenon of macroevolution at the biological level.

In the middle of the nineteenth century Charles Darwin published his *On the Origin of Species* (1859). It dealt with the development of species among animals and plants. In 1871 he published *The Descent of Man,* a study of the origin of humanity in which the human species was placed within the broad evolutionary model which he had developed into a vision of the relation between all forms of life. The central insight of Darwin is expressed in the theory of evolution by natural selection. When one looks at the alleged dynamic of this process, it appears in many ways to be re-markably wasteful. Above all it appears to be morally ambiguous at best since nature seems to select only those who are most fit to adapt to the environment. Only these will survive and beget progeny.

As this related specifically to human life, humanity was seen to emerge out of a long struggle with other species. Because of the nature of the struggle, humanity developed into the most successful form of life. The very qualities it has developed in this struggle it can now turn in the direction of struggle with other members of the human species itself. Obviously, this can easily move to a form of human, cultural evolution that legitimates the extinction of one human group by another. Those who are most fit will survive. Those who are less fit will disappear. But the idea of the survival of the fittest with the violence it seems to involve is not necessarily an au-tomatic process. Once intelligence appears on the scene, it is possible to define that which is fit in terms other than violence and in the context of a wider range of values.

It is important, however, to think of these ideas in the context of Euro-pean history in the nineteenth century. It was a time of wide-spread struggle throughout Europe to establish the national and cultural identity of the Eu-ropean peoples. It is not clear how far Darwin himself would have wished to move in the direction of interpreting the history of human culture in terms of the survival of the fittest. But, given the context of that historical period, the theory of human evolution could be incendiary in its impact. Pushed to the extreme, this will produce forms of social Darwinism that have been truly destructive in modern experience.

The most vocal advocates of evolutionary thought formulated their understanding in terms that sounded pantheistic at times and very material-istic and mechanistic at other times. Thus while Darwin's views were troublesome enough, they were developed further by others who pushed matters to a major conflict of world-views. And against this background, it is understandable that in ecclesiastical circles there was considerable hesi-tation that stood in the way of a positive conversation between theology and this new scientific theory. Two major areas of tension were obvious from the perspective of theology. The first area had to do with the reading of the opening chapters of the Bible. The second area was related to the Aristotelian world-view standing behind the major understanding of Roman Catholic theology of the time.

The more common understanding of the Scriptures saw the opening chapters of the Bible as a description of God's creative activity bringing forth the variety of creatures on earth at the beginning of history. To many Christian believers, both Protestant and Catholic, the evolutionary vision of reality seemed to stand in obvious contradiction to this view of origins in general, and to the biblical vision of human origins in particular. If evolution were to be taken seriously, it would raise the problem of a proper understanding of biblical inspiration and revelation. Thus, before we ever ask about specific matters of content, we are confronted with a major challenge to the understanding of the authority of the sacred text. Beyond this, the view of evolution raised serious questions specifically about an appropriate understanding of humanity. It was not clear how one was to speak of the question of humanity's relation to God, the problem of human responsibility, of sin, and of salvation.

One of the early steps in the history of the Catholic response to these questions may be found in the statements of the provincial synod of German bishops held in Cologne in 1860. This was prior to the publication of Darwin's book on human evolution, but it was in a context that was quite conscious of evolutionary thought patterns. The German bishops were concerned specifically with the problematic views of A. Günther and G. Hermes, both of whom were thought to hold pantheistic views concerning creation. The synod, therefore, drafted an extensive statement on the doctrine of creation. The concern with evolution appears in a statement that describes the idea that the human body is derived from the "spontaneous transformation of an inferior nature." This the bishops see as an opinion that is entirely contrary to the teaching of Scripture. Similarly, the view that doubts that the whole human race has descended from the first Adam is described as contrary to the Scriptures.[9] In assessing these statements, it is important to keep in mind that it is the concern of a provincial synod. That being the case, while it is a form of magisterial teaching, it is not to be evaluated as infallible, dogmatic teaching.

Just a few years later the agenda of Vatican Council I included a statement affirming the origin of the entire human race from a single couple.[10] It was expected that it might be defined as a dogma of faith. However the

---

[9] *Collectio Lacensis* (Freiburg: Herder, 1879) 5, 292.
[10] *Sacrorum Conciliorum Nova et Amplissima Collectio,* ed. I.D. Mansi (Arnhem & Leipzig: 1924) 50, 70; 53, 170; 53, 175.

premature closing of the Council because of the Franco-Prussian War put an end to that possibility in the context of the Council.

In 1909 the Biblical Commission published a decree on the historical character of the opening chapters of the Bible. This decree singled out the "special creation of humanity" and the "formation of the first woman from the first man" as "facts that touch the fundamentals of Christian faith."[11] While this document did not close the possibility of further research, it evoked a mood in the context of the Modernist debates of the early twentieth century that discouraged any serious theological discussion of evolution for some time.

In 1943 Pope Pius XII issued his encyclical *Divino afflante Spiritu*. This document recognizes the importance of literary form in determining the intent of the biblical texts. The encyclical was to play an important role in the subsequent development of Roman Catholic biblical studies which would open the way to significant insights into the nature of the biblical narratives at the opening of the book of Genesis. Another statement of the Biblical Commission in 1948 indicated that the earlier instructions should not be understood to exclude the re-examination of the many problems involved in scriptural interpretation. Taking these documents together, both those of the papacy and those of the Biblical Commission, we can see the significant change in the Roman Catholic church concerning the possible interpretations of the biblical texts, and corresponding to that, the change in the understanding of what is meant by the phrase *biblical inspiration*.

Another significant step appears in 1950 with the encyclical *Humani generis* of Pope Pius XII. This is a very cautiously worded statement which leaves the question of the bodily evolution of humanity open to study and discussion by experts. The task of scholars is to lay out the arguments for and against both sides of the issue. But, regardless of how the body comes into being, the encyclical maintains that the human soul is created immediately by God.[12] The encyclical also contains a strong word of warning about polygenetic forms of evolutionary theory since they seem to conflict with the doctrine of original sin and sin's universal impact on humanity.[13] Basically, this encyclical held open the possibility for study and discussion of the question of evolution among theologians.

The work of Vatican Council II did not take a position on the questions that had surfaced in theology with the rise of evolutionary thought. But the Council did speak of the change from a more static world-view to one that is more aware of the historical development of the world and of human culture. "The human race has passed from a rather static concept of reality to

[11] DS 3514.
[12] DS 3896.
[13] DS 3897.

a more dynamic, evolutionary one."[14] This section of the counciliar document on the mission of the Church for the world at large may well be seen
as a call to discuss in a fair way the new questions that have arisen for
theology because of this awareness of historical development at so many
levels. In a sense it sets the stage for the more recent statements of Pope
John Paul II who has encouraged a more positive conversation between
science and theology.

John Paul II has long taken the position that nothing stands in the way of
a rightly understood theology of creation and a rightly understood scientific theory of evolution. Evolution presupposes creation; creation, when
seen in the light of evolution, appears as an event that is carried out in time
—as a *creatio continua*—in which God comes to be seen by the eyes of
faith as the Creator of all things. The terminology of a continuing creation
to which the Pope refers has long been a part of the Christian theological
tradition as we have seen above. In the past it has been thought of mainly
as the divine creativity which, at all times, keeps the created world from
lapsing back into nothingness. This meant that it was seen largely as the
work of conserving creation. Aquinas makes the point very clearly: "The
conservation of things by God does not take place through some new sort of
act, but through the continuation of that act by which God confers being."[15]

From the side of God, the idea of continuing creation means that the act
of creation is not simply something that happens at the beginning of cosmic history. Rather, the divine creative activity is ongoing. And from the
side of creation, this means that the creature's radical dependence on the
creative action of God persists throughout the time of the creature's existence. These traditional concepts lend themselves to renewed reflection in
reference to the ongoing cosmic process through which new forms of creation come into being. God's creative power is being exercised throughout
the entire history of the cosmos. In terms of Scholastic theology, this raises
the question of the relation between God as primary cause and creatures as
active, secondary causes.

The same Pope addressed the issue again on October 22, 1996. In this
statement he referred back to *Humani generis*. He interprets the earlier
document to be saying that evolution is a serious hypothesis worthy of serious investigation and study equal to that of the opposing hypothesis. But
the situation has changed since *Humani generis* was published. Now it
seems clear that evolution is more than a hypothesis. This new papal statement speaks of a series of discoveries in various fields of knowledge that
help to confirm the basic insight of the theory of evolution. Though the

[14] *Gaudium et spes*, n. 5.
[15] *Sth*. I, 104, 1, ad 4.

Holy Father does not mention any of these specifically, we might well think of the work of paleontology, molecular biology, and especially the work of gene research. In terms of the philosophy of science, a hypothesis is simply a possible, theoretical explanation for a phenomenon whereas a theory is an explanation with some empirical evidence that begins to move in the direction of verification.

As this most recent papal statement points out, there are diverse styles of evolutionary thought. The basic insight of Darwin is the awareness that biological change, or the origin of a new species from an old one, takes place through a process of historical, biological development. Precisely what the structure of that development might be is not clear. One still hears phrases such as the "survival of the fittest" and "natural selection." Some, like Darwin himself, envision long, smooth, gradual changes; a theory of gradualism. Others more recently speak of "punctuated equilibrium." This view claims that species may experience a long period of stability broken by abrupt changes. Thus, while change seems to many scientists to be a fact, the way in which science accounts for change is not uniform. Then, even from a scientific perspective, not all scientists agree on the reality of macroevolution while most would agree on the fact of microevolution within species. What the Pope is suggesting is that these are issues that have to be decided by science, not by theology.

But there are, in fact, theories of evolution which differ at a deeper level than the above; for they reflect different philosophical assumptions. A purely materialist base would lead to an understanding of the spiritual dimension of humanity as a mere epiphenomenon of matter. Such views, writes the Pope, do not adequately ground the dignity of the human person. Here this most recent papal statement refers back to the position of Pius XII who stressed the point that, regardless of how the body comes about, the soul is created immediately by God. John Paul II now speaks of the presence of an ontological difference and of an ontological leap. The moment of transition to the spiritual may not be the object of scientific observation. But it is possible to observe signs which point to what is specific to humanity. Here the Pope speaks of the experience of metaphysical knowledge, of self-awareness and self-reflection, of moral conscience and freedom, of aesthetic and religious experience. The document ends with an unresolved question concerning the body/spirit relation, and with the insistence that theology will not be satisfied with materialist, reductionist solutions.

This document seems to have made a significant move beyond the position of Pius XII in that it is more positive in its assessment of the status of evolution as a scientific position. And, in line with other statements of John Paul II, it is a strong endorsement of conversation between science and theology in a search for some sort of consonance. It is a call for protracted dialogue. But, granted all that, the origin of the human soul remains a question with no satisfactory solution as of yet.[16]

Keeping in mind the variety of evolutionary theories, we can say that there is a widespread consensus among Roman Catholic theologians at the present time that there is no necessary contradiction between the Christian doctrine of creation and the basic conviction of evolutionary thought concerning the reality of development and variation in the realm of living creatures even at the level of macroevolution. Whether new forms of living creatures develop out of previously existing ones is an issue to be studied by science. Whether or not some form of evolution is a fact is a matter of science, not of theology. But theology, rightly understood, has the task of reflecting on the anthropological implications of such a view.

Important developments in the area of biblical studies have opened up significant new ways of reading the biblical texts, as we have seen above. And a more critical awareness of the limits of Aristotelian philosophy has opened up the possibility of developing theology through dialogue with other forms of philosophy. From the papal perspective, the serious believer is not forced to choose: either creation or evolution. These are not mutually exclusive alternatives.

There may well be conflicts with particular explanations as to how this phenomenon of evolution is to be explained, for at this level, we are no longer dealing simply with empirical data but with the shaping of theoretical constructs and with premises from a world-view espoused by the one who is interpreting the data. We have discussed this issue in greater detail in the first chapter on the relation between science and theology. Suffice it to say that such a world view may be one of hard materialism or reductionism. It may also be one of Christian faith. At this level, there may be very deep differences in understanding. It is important to realize that this is not necessarily a question of fact versus religious faith. It is, rather, a question of one sort of faith in conflict with another sort of faith.

V) *Anthropic Principle*

This would seem to be the appropriate place to raise the question of a particular style of cosmology that has arisen among scientists in the last few decades. Stated in its early form by Robert Dicke (1961) and Brandon Carter (1973), it speaks of the so-called fine-tuning of the cosmos to produce a being capable of being an observer such as we find in the case of the

---

[16] George Coyne, S.J., "Evolution and the Human Person: The Pope in Dialogue," in *Science and Theology: The New Consonance,* ed. T. Peters (Boulder, Colo.: Westview Press, 1998) 149–61.

human person. By this is meant that the conditions operative at the beginnings of cosmic history, were remarkably congenial to bring forth intelligent life. We can imagine many sorts of universes, but only where these particular conditions prevail will we find a universe that is able to bring forth beings capable of being observers of the universe. These conditions have to do, above all, with the strength of gravity and the speed of expansion in the expanding universe, as well as with the forces that bind neutrons and protons in the nucleus of the atom. If these were even minimally different, the universe would not be able to bring forth intelligent life as we know it. The properties of matter, then, at the broader cosmic level and at the smallest scale of atomic structure seem to be uniquely suited to the origin of intelligent life. From here comes the term *anthropic principle*. And it places the question of human evolution in the broadest possible cosmic framework.

Various forms of this principle have been suggested. The most common versions are known as the weak form and the strong form. The weak version argues that if humans are here, the nature of the universe must include the conditions that make the appearance of carbon-based life possible. The strong version tends to say that the structure of the universe is such that it must bring forth life.

If this is taken together with the idea of the Big Bang cosmology, two issues emerge that are problematic. The idea of a Big Bang seems to point to a beginning of the universe; the anthropic principle seems to point in the direction of some purpose involved in the universe. Both of these issues point to the outer limits of scientific methodology. The idea of a beginning that is not to be found in yet another empirical condition raises the question of an absolute or a timeless beginning. This is no longer a scientific issue, and the fact of purpose is not an empirical datum. Hence, we understand that science as science is not qualified to speak of purpose without pushing beyond its proper limits. Hence, many scientists have resisted the implications of teleology implied by the anthropic principle and have attempted to provide other explanations for the so-called fine-tuning of this universe.

With regard to theology, it is important to keep in mind that the primary concern of the idea of creation is that all things in the world, regardless of how they may appear empirically, are grounded in the creative intelligence and love of God. Theology, precisely because of its religious conviction that God creates the universe *for* something, is not uncomfortable with the implications of the anthropic principle. The point is not that the empirical data prove the existence of God.[17] That would be a new version of the

---

[17] We find such an argument in: M. J. Behe, *Darwin's Black Box: The Biochemical Challenge to Evolution* (New York: Free Press, 1996).

traditional argument for the existence of God from design. While many accounts of scientific journalism tend to move in this direction and commonly speak of science finding God,[18] few theologians are inclined to move in that direction today since it is commonly felt that it is unwise to depend on science to provide the basis of religion or theology.

Yet, while the empirical data can be employed by scientists to argue either for or against design, Christian theology itself would not be surprised to discover the signs of a creative intelligence in the workings of the created world. As we have seen above, theology has long worked with the conviction that all of creation is grounded in the intelligent, loving power of the Creator. In a series of Lenten homilies given in the Liebfrauenkirche in Munich in the 1980s, Cardinal Ratzinger spoke in response to the view of J. Monod according to which life in general and human life in particular is seen as the product of haphazard mistakes. To this Cardinal Ratzinger first states clearly that it is an issue of science to explain how the tree of life originates and continues to develop. "This is not an issue of faith. But we must have the audacity to say that the great projects of the living creation are not the products of chance and error. . . . The great projects of the living creation point to a creating Reason and show us a creating Intelligence, and they do so now more luminously and radiantly today than ever before."[19]

See doc.
Com. + flow.

---

[18] This is, in fact, the title of the cover article of *Newsweek,* July 20, 1998. The cover itself consists of what looks like a stained-glass window with two haloed figures sitting at a table. One looks into a telescope, and the other into a microscope. The outer sections of the window depict a crescent moon, a planet, and a number of characteristic scientific models of chemical structures.

[19] Cardinal Ratzinger, *"In the Beginning . . ." A Catholic Understanding of the Story of Creation and the Fall,* tr. B. Ramsey (Huntington, Ind: Our Sunday Visitor Inc., 1990) 71.

7

Sin and Evil

As we have seen in the previous chapters, the Christian tradition has a basically positive view of the created world. During the centuries, as this religious tradition engaged a variety of philosophical traditions, it encountered a number of dualistic world-views which were very suspicious of material reality, and specifically of the human body. This engagement has left its mark on subsequent Christian thought even though the tradition never gave up its ancient conviction that the world of God's creation is basically good. But despite its basic optimism, the Christian vision is quite realistic in its assessment of human experience in the world. It has never closed its eyes to the obvious painful nature of the created order even as it proclaimed the glory of God to be revealed in creation.

To the best of our knowledge, such things as earthquakes, volcanoes, floods, and other natural phenomena were part of the cosmic order long before the appearance of humanity. They could hardly be caused by human sinfulness if they antedate human existence. Nor has the tradition been blind to the monstrosities which human beings have perpetrated on one another. Warfare, ethnic cleansing, the threat of nuclear annihilation are the stuff of the daily news reports, to say nothing of the two world wars, and the Holocaust that have been a major piece of our experience in the first half of the twentieth century. How does the good creation of God come to be so marred with evil? We will never have a complete answer to such a question. But the religious tradition, going back to biblical times, has seen at least part of the answer to lie in the reality of human freedom and the destructive exercise of that human power. This is what lies at the heart of the doctrine of sin.

While St. Augustine did not create the doctrine of sin independently of the earlier Christian tradition, it is true to say that the Western tradition on the doctrine of sin has been influenced heavily by his work. And it does seem that Augustine may well have been the first to think of something like an hereditary sin and guilt. In Augustine's work the issue of sin is dealt with from the perspective of two major problematic positions; that of Manicheism and that of Pelagianism. Augustine's own theology of sin revolves largely around the interpretation of the opening texts of Genesis and the Epistle to the Romans. Both of these scriptural references are given an interpretation which has become very problematic in terms of contemporary biblical studies. This being the case, we will discuss the view of Augustine first, together with other historical concerns. This will be followed by a discussion of the contemporary understanding of the biblical material.

I) *Influence of the Interpretation of Augustine*

For nine years prior to his own baptism, Augustine had been associated with a religious movement known as Manicheism. This movement was essentially a form of metaphysical dualism that saw reality in terms of a deep conflict between good and evil, or between light and darkness. These two original principles, while separate to begin with, became intermingled as a result of a great conflict. Thus, some of the good was imprisoned in the evil. This provides a way of coming to understand the relation between material reality and spiritual reality. While spiritual reality is fundamentally good, material reality is thoroughly evil.

In terms of the material body, then, the human person is the product of the principle of evil. But the human soul springs from the realm of light. It is literally a divine particle tragically imprisoned in the evil body. It desires to gather to itself all the sparks of light that have been hidden in material beings. It is possible to rise above the material concerns of the body and live in harmony with the principle of good. This is the concern of a strict form of asceticism. Only a small number of humans would succeed in this; these were the elect. The greater number would be mere "hearers," as was Augustine himself. As a religious vision, this raises obvious questions concerning the nature of the created world, including humanity; and about any form of human agency involved in sin. Whatever evil there is in the world, it is derived from the eternal principle of evil.

At the other end of the spectrum was the view of the British monk Pelagius. In essence, his understanding seems to be naively optimistic in its outlook, at least as the view of Pelagius was taught by his disciple Coelestius. It sees human nature as basically healthy and capable of reaching its perfection by using its own resources. The human person is able to make use of freedom and is naturally capable of the most exalted moral good. There is no place in this system for the idea of a fault passed on through descent from the first human beings to subsequent generations. The sin of Adam harmed only himself, and not his descendants. Hence, anything like original sin can only mean that human beings imitate the action of Adam in their own moral decisions. Suffering, concupiscence, and death are not to be thought of as punishments for sin. They are rather elements of human nature itself in its natural condition. In view of all this, what is the point of infant baptism? It could hardly be a baptism for the remission of sin since there is no sin involved in infants. It is, rather, a sign of acceptance by the Church. Augustine fought the Pelagian position very strongly. The theory would be condemned by the bishops of North Africa in 416. It was condemned again by the Synod of Carthage in 418, and yet again by the Synod of Orange in 529.

Augustine himself was a witness to the moral decadence of the Roman Empire as well as to the threats to the empire brought by the Vandals. He died in 430, even as the Vandals were laying siege to Hippo. Taking this wider historical context into account and reflecting on Augustine's own personal struggles, it is not difficult to understand his emphasis on the pervasiveness of evil in human experience and of our apparent inability to extricate ourselves from it. This might set a helpful context for reflecting on his understanding of sin and grace.

Augustine worked on explanations of the book of Genesis at least five times during his life. This literary journey spans the years 388 to 417/418. Much of this was concerned with the problems of Manicheism. The problems raised by the Pelagians were treated in other writings done between 418 and 429. Augustine approaches the issue of Manicheism from the perspective of the question of evil. What is evil, and how does one come to understand it in the context of a world that is the work of a good Creator? Augustine's discussion was his response to the Manicheans, and it was to shape Western Christian understanding for centuries.

Contrary to the dualism of the Manicheans, Augustine begins with the premise that everything that actually exists is good.

> Behold God, and behold what God has created. God is good. Most mightily and most immeasurably does he surpass these things. But being good, he has created good things. . . . Whence, therefore, is evil, since God the supreme good, has made all these things good? He, the greater, the supreme good, has made these lesser goods, yet both creator and all created things are good.[1]

---

[1] *Confessions* 7, 5, tr. Ryan, 162–63.

God is seen to be the Supreme Good. The created order, as neo-Platonism suggests and as Augustine agrees, is a hierarchical order of degrees of goodness. While some things are better and more exalted than others, still everything that actually exists is by that fact alone to be reckoned as a good. What, then, is evil? "Evil is nothing else but the lack of the good."[2]

It is possible, then, to distinguish two types of evil. There are many things experienced in the world around us that we commonly think of as evil. Augustine will refer to these as physical evils. This category includes such things as natural disasters, sickness, suffering, etc. These can be seen to be in harmony with God's will as possible tests for the moral development of human beings. Or they may simply be what is inevitably involved in the relations between a higher and a lower level in the hierarchy of being. Here it is possible that the individual being serves the perfection of the ordered whole, and thus contributes to the beauty that arises from the polarity between contraries. It is possible that human beings suffer from such evils as a form of punishment for sin. When this is the case, it is both good and just, since it comes from the mercy of God who thus warns us.[3] Even the suffering of the innocent may be seen as rooted in human solidarity, and as possible instructions that will preserve others in goodness and grace.

The Manichean vision is undercut with the claim of Augustine that moral evil is very real, and that its cause is to be found in the created will; first that of angels, then that of human beings. The created will is situated in the context of a hierarchy of goods. Its proper inclination is to move to the higher goods, and finally to the Supreme Good. When the created will turns from the higher to the lower goods, that movement lies at the heart of sin. That to which the will turns is not evil, but the turning itself is a disordered turning to creatures rather than to the Supreme Good in which the will is to find its rest. It is possible for the will to do this because it is both finite and free. Augustine offers an example of the seriousness with which he takes human freedom:

> Take the case of two men whose physical and mental make-up is exactly the same. They are both attracted by the exterior beauty of the same person. While gazing at this loveliness, the will of one man is moved with an illicit desire; the will of the other remains firm in its purity. Why did the will become evil in one case and not in the other?. . . . And what else could be the cause of their attitudes but their own wills, since both men have the same constitution and temperament? The beauty which attracted the eyes of both was the same; the secret suggestion by which both were tempted was the same. However carefully they examine the situation,

[2] *Op. cit.,* 3, 7, 12, p. 85.
[3] *City of God,* 12, 3., tr. Walsh, etc., 247–48.

eager to learn what it was that made one of the two evil, no cause is apparent.[4]

The conclusion seems to be that the act of the will is a self-initiating act that can be reduced to nothing beyond itself. There is no point in searching for the efficient cause outside the person that makes the will to be evil. Moral evil resides essentially in the created will itself which freely disrupts the divinely willed order of good. Evil, therefore, is not grounded in some primordial evil principle as the Manicheans held. Yet, as Augustine knew from his own experience, evil is very wide-spread and persistent. He could well say with St. Paul: "For I do not do the good I want; but I do the evil I do not want" (Rom 7:19). Hence his emphasis on the need for grace.

More specifically related to the doctrine of original sin is Augustine's controversy with the Pelagians. As indicated above, Pelagius maintained the fundamental goodness of the human person, and had no use for the idea of some inherited sin or guilt. Certainly Adam had sinned. But that sin has its chief impact on subsequent generations as a bad example, and not as an inherited sin that made each of Adam's posterity to be a sinner prior to any personal moral decisions of the individual. Already St. Ambrose had used the Roman legal recognition of the *pater familias* and his relation to his posterity. Since such a person was legally the head of the household, his actions, whether good or bad, could have an impact on the whole of his family. This could involve such things as being liberated from slavery or being placed into slavery. Ambrose, and Augustine following the lead of Ambrose, would use this idea as a means of expressing the relation between Adam and his posterity. With such a legal structure, it is not difficult to think of an inherited guilt.

From that perspective Augustine can look at the description of Adam and Eve in the Garden of Eden. While Augustine will commonly develop spiritual understandings of this biblical material, it is clear that behind such understandings is his conviction that these two human beings are the real, historical ancestors of the human race. Clearly, the garden is also real as are the gifts with which the first humans were endowed. There was the supernatural gift of original justice, and there were the preternatural gifts of knowledge, integrity, immortality, etc. When we think of Augustine's Adam prior to the Fall, he was, indeed, uniquely endowed. So much is this the case that it becomes difficult to understand how he could have fallen into sin. But he did fall, and all his posterity bear the impact of his act. Augustine argues strongly for the idea of hereditary guilt.

In a very sharply focused synthesis of his understanding of the first sin and its impact on subsequent generations, Augustine writes:

---

[4] *Op. cit.,* 12, 6, p. 252–53.

> God, the Author of all natures but not of their defects, created man good;
> but man, corrupt by choice and condemned by justice, has produced a
> progeny that is both corrupt and condemned. For we all existed in that
> one man, since taken together, we were the one man who fell into sin
> through the woman who was made out of him before sin existed. Al-
> though the specific form by which each of us was to live was not yet cre-
> ated and assigned, our nature was already present in the seed from which
> we were to spring. And because this nature has been soiled by sin and
> doomed to death and justly condemned, no human being was to be born
> in the human race in any other condition.[5]

The relation between Adam and the rest of the human race is seen here in
terms of the theory of seminal reasons. This can be seen to provide a biological background for the understanding of legal responsibility spoken of
above.

An obvious scriptural text supporting this viewpoint is found in the
Epistle to the Romans. In the Latin translation in use at that time, we find
the basis for the following: "Therefore, just as sin entered the world through
one man . . . in whom all have sinned. . . ." (Rom 5:12). It is now recognized that the Latin translation involved here is an erroneous rendering of
the original Greek; but at the time of Augustine, it was the Latin text that
was in use. And it is easy to see how this could be taken to imply some
form of hereditary guilt. It was in this sense that Augustine saw it, and his
interpretation would have enduring impact on Western Christian understanding. There are, therefore, two realities to be distinguished in speaking
of original sin. There is the primal sin of the first Adam *(peccatum origi-
nans);* and there is the inherited impact of that sin in his posterity *(peccatum originatum).* In the idea of an inherited sin, Augustine would see the
key to understanding his own experience which seemed to resonate with
that of St. Paul.

One seems to be strongly inclined toward evil almost independently of
one's will. The pervasive human experience of disordered desire or concupiscence, especially in the form of disordered sexual desire, may be seen as
an experiential confirmation of Augustine's theology of an inherited sin.
Because of the sin of Adam, all human beings have become a God-forsaken
mass of humanity *(massa damnata, massa perditionis)* and are subject to
death. In such a context, we can see the logic of his insistence on the necessity of grace in human life and on the importance of infant baptism. For
an infant dying in the state of original sin, there is no hope of heaven. If the
infant dies before receiving baptism, its fate is damnation.

[5] *Op. cit.,* 13, 14, p. 278–79.

II) *The Council of Trent*

The teaching of the Council of Trent is best approached by keeping in mind two major movements of that time. On the one hand, it was the time of the great Renaissance in European culture. Simply looking at the name of this movement, one might be tempted to ask what was reborn at this time? Looking at the art and literature of the period, the answer to that question might well be that some of the values of pagan antiquity were reborn, now in the form of an optimistic humanism which focused strongly on the nobility and native goodness of humanity. If we look at the period in terms of the theological history we have just discussed above, we might qualify our answer by saying that it is also a period of the rebirth of Pelagianism. In terms of theology, a person who is deeply involved in the humanism of Renaissance will be inclined to think of original sin not as something that lurks deep down in the core of the person, but rather in terms of extrinsic imputation.

On the other hand, it is the time of the great Protestant Reformation movement. This was a religious movement that saw humanity in much more negative terms. Impressed with some of the very negative language of Augustine, Reformation theology is inclined to speak of the depth of human corruption. Luther, much like Augustine in this respect, spoke out of his own experience. The human will seems to be the slave of lower desires. Concupiscence never seems to leave one, no matter how hard one tries. Concupiscence is identical with original sin. How, then, does one find a merciful God? The answer to that lies in the area of a trusting faith. Recognize the depth of your sinfulness, and place yourself in the hands of a loving, merciful God. This is related to a positive doctrine of forensic justification. Because of the merits of Jesus, God declares the sinner to be just even though sin remains deep within.

The Council of Trent lists the errors which are its concern. They are Pelagianism, the humanistic views of Erasmus, the humanistic doctrine of Albert Pighius, and the theology of Martin Luther. The basic question, then, is: How deeply do the realities of grace and sin touch the human person? Do they both touch the person only on the surface, or do they reach also to the depth of one's personal center?

Trent makes it clear that its view of original sin is different from that of the Reformation and from that of the Pelagians. In contrast with such views, Trent teaches that by his transgression of the divine command, Adam lost the sanctity and justice in which he had been constituted; and that, because of this sin, the whole Adam was changed for the worse, in body and in soul. The sin of Adam is passed on to all human beings by the mere fact of being born into the human race *(propagatione)* prior to any personal sinful action *(non imitatione)*. Human freedom is not destroyed by this sinful condition, though it is weakened. But, contrary to the view of Reformation theology and to the very different view of the Pelagians, the sacrament of baptism removes the guilt of original sin by reason of the grace of Jesus Christ, though it does not heal human concupiscence which remains even after baptism. Concupiscence itself, however, is not to be identified with sin, though it comes from sin and inclines one to sin.

The Council expressly states that it does not wish to include the case of the Blessed Virgin Mary in its statement when it teaches that all humans after Adam are born without the gift of that original grace and justice which God intended for humanity. This means that, prior to any personal ethical decision, each human person (with the exception of the Blessed Virgin) is interiorly affected in the moral-religious sphere of personal existence by the mere fact of being born into the human community. This is seen to be a real state of alienation from God in contrast to mere extrinsic imputation. Yet it is not to be confused with personal, free sin. And this state of alienation can be overcome only through the redemptive work of Jesus Christ. The Tridentine position reflects the older traditional understanding of grace as a divine gift that reaches into the depths of the human person and leads to an ongoing transformation of the person, called in the Greek tradition divinization, and in some cases in the medieval West, deification. And if grace reaches this deeply into the human person, so also does the reality of sin. Neither can be limited to good or bad example coming at the person from the outside.

III) *Contemporary Interpretations of Scripture*

Early in this century the statements of the Biblical Commission discouraged the serious critical study of the biblical texts involved in dealing with original sin. Several documents refer emphatically to the historical character of the opening chapters of Genesis. This conviction is repeated by Pius XII in *Humani generis*. But as other magisterial statements encouraged the use of critical methods without condoning any specific conclusions to be drawn on the basis of these methods, it became possible for Catholic biblical scholars to look at these texts in a new way, and to draw fresh insights into their deep, religious meaning.

The negative side of this movement involves the realization that the style of interpretation which we have described, at least from the time of Augustine, can no longer be sustained. For centuries it was assumed by theologians and by magisterial statements that Adam and Eve were the names of real, individual people at the beginning of human history, and that they first lived in truly paradisal conditions endowed with the gifts of grace and the many other gifts described by Augustine. Then for some puzzling reason, these two first human beings collaborated in the downfall of the human race. These convictions stand in the background of the language-style with which theology has spoken of "the Fall" for centuries, even at the level of the teaching of the Council of Trent. To speak of this as a common conviction or presupposition is not the same as saying that it is defined, dogmatic teaching of the Church. But it is the perspective from which the language of the Tridentine teaching is shaped.

One issue of contemporary exegesis that stands out is the conviction that the first three chapters of Genesis should not be read in isolation, but should be taken within the larger context of biblical thought. Some of the issues that emerge from this broader context have to do with the deeply relational character of humanity and the historical development of the mystery of sin and of grace in Jewish and more broadly in human experience.

The biblical theology of sin would be inconceivable without an awareness of the deeply relational understanding of humanity that is so pervasive in the biblical literature of both Testaments. We have seen this already in the second chapter of this book where we discussed the understanding of the book of Genesis. There humanity was seen in terms of a particular relation with God on the one side, and an intimate relation to the rest of the created order on the other side.

It is not surprising, therefore, to see that the account of human failure, beginning with Genesis 3 and going to Genesis 11, appears as a history of damaged or broken relations. First there is the loss of intimacy with God. Then comes the description of broken relations among humans, and the painful relation of humanity to the non-human world.

The accounts of sin found here must be read in the broader context of the Jewish theology of a divinely willed covenant. In contrast with the blessings to be expected in a covenanted world, the experience of the people has been that of a long and painful history. "When the Lord saw how great was man's wickedness on the earth, and how no desire that his heart conceived was ever anything but evil, he regretted that he had made man on the earth, and his heart was grieved" (Gen 6:5-6). The Jewish experience of a world distorted and torn by human actions provides the key for reflecting on the wider human situation. Not only has the Jewish experience been one of a world very different from the divinely willed order, but the same is true of humanity broadly.

The sense of universalism becomes very clear in the period of the monarchy. "For there is no one who does not sin" (1 Kg 8:46). The prophets never tire of crying out against the persistent tendency of the people to choose evil rather than good. Comparing the city of Jerusalem to a woman, Jeremiah writes:

> If you ask in your heart why these things befall you; for your great guilt
> your skirts are stripped away and you are violated. Can the Ethiopian
> change his skin, the leopard his spots? As easily would you be able to do
> good, accustomed to evil as you are " (Jer 13:22-23).

In the light of the best contemporary biblical studies, therefore, it becomes clear that the text of Genesis 3 should probably not be read as a description of a single event at the beginning of human history. In what sense can we still speak of history? It might well be seen as an aetiological account that provides theological insight into the historical condition of humanity which has been generated, at least in part, by the exercise of human freedom. The Genesis text should not be read as an account based on eye witness reports or carefully kept records. It is not history in that sense. But the author of the text is facing the painful, twisted moral situation of humans from the perspective of the specifically Jewish experience of history. A major piece of that Jewish history is the conviction that God is a God of saving presence, who wills covenant with this people. God is a God of promise, and the promise is of people and a land in which to live. But for centuries of Jewish history, the fulfillment of this promise has been fragmentary at best, and constantly threatened.

How is one to understand this polarity between God's will for covenant and the painful experience of the people of covenant? The answer to this question raises the issue of human infidelity in response to God. This actual experience of the Jewish people is the point of departure for understanding the Genesis material. While a variety of symbols and myths shared with other religious traditions may stand in the background, the point of Genesis is not to speak of a timeless truth of human nature as many myths do. The real point is to describe the historical roots of the present situation. The present may be seen in the past, and the past in the present. That which appears to be the first sin is the first in a series, as we have seen above. Human history seems to be infested with this problem wherever we look. It is not only a Jewish experience; it is a broader human experience. The Jews as a people do not yet exist in this pre-Abrahamic material.

The major point of Genesis could be put as follows. The God of creation is a God of goodness; and creation, as the work of this God, is good. It is the expression of God's love and beneficence. The problems which we experience in history, therefore, are not caused by some sort of divine carelessness much less divine impotence. Rather, the negative pole of historical experience is to be traced, at least in part, to free, human choices. So it is now; and so it seems always to be.

Thus the narrative of Genesis 3 can well be read as a description of the human tendency to push against limits. In this case, it can be seen as an attempt to take on the divine function of arbitrating good and evil. When humans have the audacity to take over this divine function, their world begins to fall apart—then and now. That which begins in Genesis reaches a climactic point in the building of the tower of Babel and the confusion of tongues. We read this not as a story about the origin of languages, but as a description of the human inability to communicate. The Genesis story is the biblical equivalent of the myth of Prometheus who steals the fire of the gods. And for this the mythic hero must pay dearly. Similarly, in the biblical account, humanity has freely chosen a condition of alienation from God. For this humanity pays dearly.

Is this story true? We need only look at the constant experience of human history; the twisted character of human relations with others and with the entire world of creation, and the moral ambiguity so pervasive in human history. Tragic events in the history of the twentieth century bear eloquent testimony to the remarkable realism of the biblical vision. This is not God's creation as God would have it. This is the result of human, free choices.

IV) *Sin and the Contemporary Context*

What are some of the issues that might be raised for theology in the light of the contemporary sciences? It seems that the entire picture of the idyllic state at the beginning of history and the figure of Adam as a giant of human perfection become impossible if one thinks of a cosmos beginning as the Big Bang envisions it, and gradually developing to new and not always better forms. The idea of paradisal beginnings of peace and harmony followed by a history of tragedy is hard to envision even if we do not think of evolution as a process of inevitable improvement. How are we to think of the first human parents in the context of modern paleontology? The evidence usually appealed to in support of evolution points to early humans in what seem to be primitive conditions. It is difficult to envision the ethical giant that seems to be involved in the traditional understanding of Adam, gifted with grace and a cluster of gifts that would make him far superior to humans even today. This does not seem to be a coherent theological position.

It might be helpful, in this context, to recall the thought of Irenaeus of Lyons. His image of Adam is that of an infant in the infancy of the human race. The challenge for Adam is to grow into a fuller, more mature, personal love of God. The failure of Adam to do so is what lies at the heart of the Fall. That is, the Fall is not so much a loss of a perfect and complete past as much as it is the failure to move appropriately to the perfecting and completing future.

Might it be better to think of the paradisal descriptions of origins not as a picture of how things began but rather as a symbol of the future to which God, the Creator, is calling creation? If that is possible, then what we tend to think of as biblical protology is better approached as eschatology. It is a symbol that elicits the sense of a world that has never yet existed, but that remains an object of hope for the future. If we view the text from the perspective of the history of grace directed to the fulfillment which it has reached in Christ, then it is possible to think of the history of sin as the collaborative human failure to move in the direction of God's aim as revealed in Christ.

This need not mean that the early humans had any explicit knowledge of God's aim. But we can understand it to mean that as human beings emerged to levels of knowledge and freedom, they carried with them much of their pre-human rootage together with the mechanisms of survival. But the call of God to the future is a call to move beyond such mechanisms as a way of structuring human life together and to move in the direction of what Christ reveals as self-sacrificing love. The failure to make that move leads to the creation of structural, social rigidities that make it difficult to move in the direction that God intends for creation. Obviously this human process must have begun somewhere. But what we know theologically as the Fall is not an affair of a single individual at the dawning of history. It is rather the failure of early generations, wherever they may have emerged, and of subsequent generations down to the present.

The Fall, then, is the collaborative failure of humanity to move appropriately beyond its primitive rootage to a level of freely chosen love in response to the creative love of God. We might want to reflect on this in relation to the ethical implications of the emergence of humanity as an intelligent and free creature in an evolving world. As Karl Rahner and others have pointed out, the human creature is the process of biological evolution at a point where it can take the process of development into its own hands, make specific value judgments, and perhaps even change the direction of the process in relation to specifically human choices. We might suggest, then, that what the sciences know as evolution by natural selection will be replaced by evolution through human intervention. Whether such human choices will be appropriate to move the history of the cosmos to the most perfect fulfillment of God's initial aim remains to be seen. God has created a world of such a sort that the realization of the divine aim depends on the reaction of God's human creatures. Seen from this perspective, the seriousness of sin is not diluted by evolutionary thought. Rather human freedom and ethical consciousness become all the more important.

What is one to think of the obviously painful character of the world in which we find ourselves? From certain perspectives, the created cosmos is truly a thing of beauty that can easily move one to a sense of wonder and awe. But it is not simply a world of unmitigated beauty. It is also a world profoundly marked by the struggle for life. All around us, and even in ourselves and in our relation to each other, we find that life comes from life. This means that some living creature must die so that another one might live a healthy life. There is a pervasive movement to more and fuller life which moves through pain, struggle, and death. It seems, particularly at the level of life, that the world operates on principles that are very painful.

If we think of Christ as the embodiment of the cosmic word, we might ask: Does the figure of the man on a cross suggest the deeper significance of what we find in the cosmos—or at least on our planet—at every level? Simply put, the revelation of the created order is ambiguous. Pain and struggle seem to be built into the structure of the cosmos as it moves toward life in a variety of forms. We seem to be confronted with perpetual perishing, as Whitehead once wrote. New life comes from what looks like destruction. Are lower forms of life simply destroyed, or are they transformed as they are taken up into higher life? Is suffering, perhaps, the key to moving to something higher? Can we see this as an anticipation at the cosmic level of what is most clearly affirmed in the experience of Jesus and the cross?

Might it be helpful, again, to move in a direction suggested already by Irenaeus of Lyons. God creates a world filled with challenges so that human beings, in meeting those challenges, will be able to grow and develop into their full potential? Can we see these challenges as pointing to a world that is marked by the pain of the cross? This finds its most express statement in the cross of Christ.

Looking at that figure in Christian terms, we can say that the creative power that undergirds all cosmic reality is enacted in Christ as personal, self-sacrificing love. That which generates and sustains cosmic reality, including humanity, and draws out its ever new forms of being is a power that is loving, personal, forgiving, and fulfilling. We find that for human beings the appropriate way of relating with each other and with the world around them is through the ethics of self-giving love, even though the world operates on the basis of other principles in other dimensions.

8

Christ and the Cosmos

There is a rich form of cosmic christology in the Christian tradition which, for the most part, has been forgotten. This form of christological reflection has its roots in the Scriptures. It is developed in the era of the Fathers of the church and is found in strong forms well into the twelfth and thirteenth centuries. Some of the biblical texts that pertain to this we have seen already in chapter 3 above. We can single out the following: 1 Cor 8:6; Eph 1:3-14; Col 1:15-20; Phil 2:6-11; Heb 1:1-4; John 1:1-14. Elements in these texts that would find significant development in later theologians have to do with the relation of Christ to creation in the primordial mystery of God's creative purpose, and with the factual, historical obstacles to the realization of that purpose which are the stuff of human sinfulness. These seminal scriptural insights would be developed further by later Christian writers.

Already in the *Shepherd of Hermas* we find indications of a christological orientation to creation theology. "The Son of God was born before all his creation, so as to be counselor to the Father about creation" (*Similitude,* IX, 12, 2).[1] And even more in the following where the salvific function of the Son is developed together with the creative function:

> The name of the Son of God is mighty and uncontained, and sustains the whole world. So if all creation is sustained by the Son of God, what do you think about those called by him, bearing the name of the Son of God, and proceeding according to his commandments. Do you see which ones he sustains? Those who bear his name with all their heart. He became

[1] *Shepherd . . . ,* 230.

their foundation and sustains them gladly because they are not ashamed
to bear his name (*Similitude,* IX, 14, 5-6).[2]

In the following we shall reflect on one author from a very early period
of Christian history. This will be followed by a discussion of one school of
reflection in the medieval period. Then we will look of the work of one
contemporary author and draw some conclusions.

I) *Irenaeus of Lyons*

In an effort to respond to the Gnostics of his time, Irenaeus of Lyons (d.
202) developed an impressive theology of history. Problematic elements of
the Gnostic position related to a dualistic understanding of history and a
dualistic understanding of matter and spirit. Concerning the first, the Gnostic view distinguished the Jewish revelatory history from the Christian history. History from creation to Christ is related to a demiurge, which is
identified with the God of the Hebrew Testament. The God of the Christian
Testament is superior to the demiurge of the Hebrew Testament. Concerning matter and spirit, the Gnostic view saw material reality as a movement
away from the primordial oneness. Materiality, therefore, is something to
be transcended. There is in the human person a spiritual element that
yearns for God, but the fulfillment of that yearning is impeded by the material body and the material world in which it is situated. In this context,
salvation is thought of as a liberation from the lower, material elements
with which the spiritual element is united. Thus, Gnosticism involves a
problem both in its understanding of history and in its understanding of
creation.

The response of Irenaeus is laid out in a Christ-centered vision of history moving from creation to eschatological fulfillment. The Epistle to the
Ephesians provides the central idea around which this entire theology is
developed:

> In all wisdom and insight, he has made known to us the mystery of his will
> in accord with his favor that he set forth in him as a plan for the fullness of
> times, to sum up all things in Christ, in heaven and on earth (1:9-10).

The Greek word that names this action of God in Christ is translated into
English with the single word *recapitulate*. Thus, as God's original plan was
that all things would be directed to Christ, so salvation would mean that the
primal unity destroyed by sin would be restored. All will be returned to
unity under the headship of Christ.

[2] *Op. cit.,* 231–32.

This means, for Irenaeus, that the two Testaments do not involve two distinct divine principles, one better than the other. Rather, it is the same God and the same Word of God who has been active throughout the whole of history. The God who creates is the God who saves. The created world, then, is not the result of some primordial tragedy. It is, rather, the work of a loving God who creates through the mediation of the pre-existent Word. Why does God create? Not because God has any need for a created world, but out of pure love. "It is not as though God had need of human beings; but rather (God creates), so as to have someone on whom to confer the divine gifts."[3] God creates a world with human beings in it so as to have personal creatures capable of receiving and responding to the gift of the divine self-communication. God creates through the Word, and it is the same Word that becomes flesh and brings the order of creation to its final fulfillment in the transformation of the resurrection.

The biblical history prior to Christ is the divine education of humanity, preparing it for the coming of Christ. In his history, the incarnate Word reenacts and lifts to a higher level all that has gone before. In this sense, he recapitulates the course of the first creation in order to restore it and elevate it. There is an active power in Christ which makes it possible for him to take into himself all the historical stages that precede him in order to transform the whole of history and bring it to a new level of fulfillment.

Here emerges another basic idea in Irenaeus' theology. It is the idea of *growth*. The first creation begins not as a perfect world but as a world laden with potential for growth. It is to grow to maturity, and in that will be its fulfillment. Corresponding to a world in its infancy, the first human beings are created as infants in the infancy of the human race. They were to grow through a history of response to God's grace and to advance to an ever deeper resemblance to their Creator. The incarnate Word, then, enters history as an infant and passes through all the stages of creaturely growth to reach the full potential of creation in the mystery of the resurrection. Thus, God recapitulates all of creation and history in the mystery of the incarnate Word. If we think of creation from this perspective, we can conclude that, in the view of Irenaeus, the mystery of creation is aimed at the sort of fulfillment which Christians believe has taken place in the person and destiny of Jesus Christ. Creation, then, may be seen as a preparation for that sort of kinship between God and humanity that has been realized in the mystery of Christ. The strong linear vision of a Christ-centered history, inspired by the texts of St. John and St. Paul, holds together the mystery of creation, of salvation, and of final consummation. All is seen with Christ as the unifying point.

[3] *Adversus haereses* IV, 14.

II) *Medieval Approaches*

Western soteriological tradition since the medieval period has been dominated by various interpretations of the work of St. Anselm. In its most common form, this is a theology that sees the mystery of the incarnation not in terms of creation-theology, but solely in terms of its relation to salvation in a world riddled with sin. In one of its most pointed formulations of the question, the medieval world could ask: Would the Word have become flesh if Adam had not sinned? That is, if we try to envision the order of creation prior to and independently of the sin of humanity, would such a thing as an incarnation of the divine Word have played any role in it? If we wish to give an affirmative answer to such a question, how would we deal with the creed that describes the incarnation as taking place "for us human beings, and for our salvation?" In medieval terms, this is the question of the motive of the incarnation.

If we follow the inspiration of Aquinas' systematization of the Anselmian theology of vicarious satisfaction, we will be inclined to think of the original divine plan for creation to be independent of the mystery of Christ. It is because of the Fall of Adam that God enacts a second plan that includes the mystery of the incarnation for the sake of human redemption. Thus, for this viewpoint, the primary motive for the incarnation of the Word was the redemption of humanity. This being the case, there would have been no incarnation had humanity not fallen into sin. In technical language, this is known as the theory of the conditioned predestination of the incarnation.[4]

While Scripture can easily be cited to support this theory, there is another view that appears already in the East in the work of Maximus Confessor (d. 662). He had espoused the idea that Christ was the goal of creation, and that the Word would have become incarnate even if there had been no sin. In the West, a strong bond between creation and salvation is found in the work of Rupert of Deutz (d. 1142). He saw the emanation of the Son from the Father as a mystery that was related to the mediatorial role of the divine Word in the work of creation. And beyond this, he argues that the incarnation of the Word is included in God's eternal plan for creation. This view would be supported commonly though not exclusively by theologians of the Franciscan Order.

This orientation finds its most articulate formulation in the work of John Duns Scotus. But the way is laid out in advance by other friars such as Bonaventure and Matthew of Aquasparta. In its final Scotistic form, it is known as the theory of the absolute or unconditional primacy of Christ. The core of this tradition can be expressed in the following way.

---

[4] *Sth* III, 1, 3.

The cosmos without Christ would somehow be incomplete. Therefore one speaks of the unconditional predestination of Christ. This relates to the conviction that the Word became flesh not because humans had sinned, but rather because God wished to share the mystery of the divine life and love and beauty as fully as possible with a creature. And that is the primary meaning of the mystery of Christ. In this sense, God's aim in creating is so that Christ may come to be. The conclusion, then, is that with or without sin, the incarnation is God's initial aim in creating and would have taken place even if sin had never entered the picture. But when sin does become a factor, the modality of the incarnation changes. Because of sin, we see the actual incarnation taking place in the mode of a suffering, crucified, and glorified Christ. That is, the incarnation takes place in such a way as to overcome the humanly constructed obstacles to achieving God's first aim: the sharing of divine life and love with creation.

The scriptural base to which this theory will appeal is found above all in the Pauline tradition. Those texts which seem to make the incarnation dependent on the reality of sin are interpreted in terms of the actual, historical experience of the incarnation which, in fact, takes place in a fallen world. For this tradition the incarnation does, indeed, have a redemptive function with respect to sin. But precisely in achieving this function, it simultaneously serves to bring the created world to its God-intended end.

In the view of a medieval theologian such as Bonaventure, the figure of Christ is the convergence of all that makes up created reality together with the mystery of the divine, present in Christ as the incarnate Word. Thus in speaking of the cosmic meaning of the incarnation of the Word, Bonaventure writes as follows: In the incarnation "the perfection of the entire created order is realized, for in that one being (= Christ) the unity of all reality is brought to consummation."[5] In Bonaventure's view the figure of Christ is the synthesis of created materiality and created spirit together with the uncreated mystery of God in the person of the divine Word. We are dealing with a tradition, therefore, that sees in the Christ-mystery a statement about the religious significance of the material, created universe. This, as we have seen already, has strong roots in the earlier biblical tradition of God's involvement in the world and in its history.

We can think of this theological vision in terms of three texts of Bonaventure. The first is taken from his theological miniature entitled *On the Reduction of the Arts to Theology*. This text describes the relation of creation to Christ from the bottom up. Thus, matter is seen not as something totally inert, but as having an active appetite upward for union with spirit.

---

[5] Hayes, Z., *What Manner of Man? Sermons on Christ by St. Bonaventure* (Chicago: Franciscan Herald Press, 1974) 74.

Such a union takes place in humanity. But even that noble form of creation is not the end of the picture; for creation in humanity is open to yet another possibility; that of union with the uncreated Word of God in whom all the "Ideas" of created things are contained. When this union of the uncreated Word, created spirit, and matter takes place, it is there that we find the most perfect realization of the potential of the created order.[6] In this text no mention is made of sin and redemption. It is purely a theology of creation.

The second text is from one of Bonaventure's Christmas sermons. It is based on the prologue of John's Gospel. It is cast in terms of the understanding of antiquity which thought of the circle as a perfect figure which can be used by Christian theology to unite the mystery of origins with that of completion. This figure, then, can be used to elicit a sense of the perfection of the universe. Bonaventure writes as follows:

> Now, if this figure (= that of creation emanating from God) is to be as perfect as possible, the line of the universe must be curved into a circle. Indeed, God is simply the First. And the last in the world of creation is humanity. Therefore, when God became human, the works of God were brought to perfection. This is why Christ, the God-man, is called the Alpha and the Omega, the beginning and the end. For this reason, as you have heard, the last of creation, namely humanity, is said to be the first and the last. This perfection in the order of nature must be properly understood. The ability of human nature to be united in unity of person with the divine—which is the most noble of all the receptive potencies implanted in human nature—is brought to act so that it would not be a mere empty potency. And when it is reduced to act (= in Christ), the perfection of the entire created order is realized, for in this one being, the unity of all reality is brought to consummation.[7]

The third text is taken from a sermon on the feast of the transfiguration. The same material is found in Bonaventure's commentary on Luke's Gospel. In Bonaventure's eyes the transfiguration is to be seen as an anticipation of the resurrection; and as such, it points to the total transformation of the created universe in Christ that lies in the future.

> All things are said to be transfigured in the transfiguration of Christ in as far as something of each creature was transfigured in Christ. For in His human nature, Christ has something in common with all creatures. With the stone He shares existence; with plants He shares life; with animals, He shares sensation; and with the angels, He shares intelligence. Therefore, all things are said to be transformed in Christ since, by virtue of His

---

[6] *De reductione artium*, #22.
[7] Hayes, *op. cit.*, 74.

humanity, He embraces something of every creature in Himself when He is transfigured.[8]

It is clear in Bonaventure that the whole of the universe serves humanity in the fullest sense by awakening humans to an awareness of the creative love of God. The human race, on the other hand, has as its most basic function that of giving conscious and loving praise to the mystery of God in the name of the entire universe. Humanity, then, is that point at which the created universe is most deeply open to the mystery of God, and capable of the deepest kind of transforming union with the divine. When this potential is fulfilled in the preeminent sense that is realized in Christ, it is at that point that the creative aim of God is brought to fulfillment. But Christ does not stand alone. In His individual destiny He anticipates the destiny of all. Thus, for this tradition, creation is ordered to Christ—to the incarnation— as to its final cause. A world transformed in Christ is what God's creative love intends from all eternity.

The Franciscan tradition of cosmic Christology found its most explicit formulation in the work of John Duns Scotus. It is here that we meet the most emphatic statement of the idea of the absolute predestination of Christ. For Scotus, that which God first intends in creating is the reality of Christ as the center of the universe. Christ is what God had in mind in shaping the rest of the universe. It is only in a secondary sense that Christ is thought of as the redeemer of the fallen human race. Thus, for Scotus, all grace is somehow related to Christ, even the grace of the first humans in their original innocence. In speaking of Christ's predestination to glory, Scotus says:

> . . . it does not seem to be solely because of the redemption that God predestined this soul (i.e., that of Christ) to such glory, since the redemption or the glory of the souls to be redeemed is not comparable to the glory of the soul of Christ. Neither is it likely that the highest good in the whole of creation is something that merely chanced to take place, and that only because of some lesser good. Nor is it probable that God predestined Adam to such a good before he predestined Christ.[9]

Viewed from the perspective of orderly love, genuine love embraces the good precisely in its goodness, and not as a means to something else. It would be contrary to the wisdom of God to love the supreme good only as a means to an end and not as an end in itself. Since the supreme good in all creation is the mystery of Christ, the perfect lover of the divine, God wills

---

[8] *Sermon I for the second Sunday of Lent* (IX, 218).
[9] A. Wolter, *Duns Scotus: Four Questions on Mary* <Intr.,text, and trans.> (Santa Barbara, Calif.: 1988) 30–31.

Christ precisely as that supreme good, and not first as a means to human salvation.

III) *Teilhard de Chardin*

If we ask about any historical antecedents for the theological vision of Teilhard de Chardin, we may look to the Johannine and Pauline tradition in Scripture. It would be interesting also to ask about some striking affinities between Teilhard's work and the theology of the medieval Franciscans which we have just discussed. In approaching Teilhard's work, we are concerned primarily with two areas: (1) Why does God create? and (2) How does Christ enter into God's plan for creation.

There is a striking parallel between the Franciscan tradition and the vision of Teilhard. But at the level of the physical world-view, the medieval theologians differ dramatically from Teilhard. Clearly, Scotus and other medieval theologians developed their theology in the context of the Aristotelian understanding of the cosmos. This is a world-view concerned principally about stability and permanence, and not so much with the dynamic of change. This world-view, however, is not part of the content of biblical revelation. Nor is it the world-view that seems to lurk behind the texts of Genesis. It is rather the context of scientific understanding available to the authors of that time as a description of what the cosmos looks like, and how it operates.

For Teilhard this seemed no longer to be a viable physical world-view. But if that is the case, how can we think about this theological vision in the context of a different world-view? For Teilhard, this must be the view of a developmental cosmos, as it was beginning to appear to the sciences at the time he was active. More specifically, the primary issue was triggered by his conviction concerning the evolution of humanity, and its place in the universe at large. In the introduction to the *Divine Milieu*, Teilhard writes:

> The enrichment and ferment of religious thought in our time has undoubtedly been caused by the revelation of the immensity and unity of the world all around us and within us. All around us, the physical sciences are endlessly extending the abyss of time and space, and ceaselessly discerning new relationships between the elements of the universe. Within us, a whole world of affinities and inter-related sympathies, as old as the human soul, is being awakened by the stimulus of these great discoveries, and what has hitherto been dreamed rather than experienced is at last taking shape and consistency. . . . It is almost a commonplace today to find people who, quite naturally and unaffectedly, live in the explicit consciousness of being an atom or a citizen of the universe.[10]

---

[10] *Divine Milieu*, (New York: Harper & Row, 1960) 13.

We might well wonder, was this really written in the 1920s? It could well serve as a summary statement of the present moment. About humanity, Teilhard writes:

> We live at the center of the network of cosmic influences as we live at the heart of the human community or among the myriads of stars, without alas, being aware of their immensity. If we wish to live our humanity and our Christianity to the full, we must overcome this lack of sensibility which tends to conceal things from us in proportion as they are too close to us or too vast. It is worth while performing the salutary exercise which consists in starting from the most personalized zones of our consciousness and following the prolongations of our being throughout the world. We shall be astonished at the extent and the intimacy of our relationship with the universe.[11]

At the root of Teilhard's vision is the idea that the process of becoming in the cosmos is a process of union. Union leads not to fusion, but to differentiation. We are then confronted with a vision of the increasing convergence and complexification of cosmic elements. Through this process, gradually consciousness develops. Thus, the simple chemistry of pre-life eventually moves to life; life moves to conscious life. Conscious life moves to freely formed life in community, and all of this converges around what Teilhard calls an Omega point, using the last letter of the Greek alphabet to designate the final fruit of the process.

At this point we are speaking of what Teilhard sees from a scientific view-point. This is his scientific model. The names for these stages of development are: geogenesis—biogenesis—psychogenesis—noogenesis. Seen in these terms, the process can be described as a process of personalization and socialization; and its basic law is that of union. Complexification leads to consciousness. It is interesting to think of the parallels and differences between this model and some of the current scientific convictions about the operation of the cosmos. There is a form of complexification theory in current literature. And though many might have trouble with the apparently too-straight line from cosmic elements to the emergence of human life in Teilhard's vision, it has a certain similarity to current forms of what is called anthropic cosmology which we discussed above.

Whatever one says about such things, it is important to point out that Teilhard sees the cosmos to be thoroughly drenched with an almost magnetic energy that takes the form of a universal attraction to unite. As union becomes more complex, it is linked to a developing inwardness. This cosmic energy is operative at all levels, beginning with that of simple chemical interactions. When we find it at the level of human experience, it takes

[11] *Op. cit.*, 27.

on personal characteristics involving consciously, freely chosen values and goals. Here it is called love. Can we then use that designation in an analogous sense to name that cosmic power at every level?

In this way Teilhard comes to envision love as a cosmic energy. It is an expression of the basic affinity of one being for another. As new and richer levels of being emerge in the cosmic process, this power can be seen as a transforming energy. Thus, Teilhard's vision of a developing universe is a vision of the transformation of the world through the power of love, and love can be likened to fire. The image of fire stands for the warmth and radiance of love and light as well as the fusion and the transformation of the elements. It is the most universal, the most powerful, and the most mysterious of cosmic energies. It is central to his understanding of personalization and socialization.

This should make it clear how Teilhard envisions the movement of matter toward spirit as one of transformation. And if we are willing to admit that, in the end, a process derives its most proper name from its final fruit, we can say at this point that the process that begins with geogenesis is finally to be named anthropogenesis. It brings forth that form of conscious, intelligent life that can freely choose its form of communal existence. It brings forth the human community.

With this as a working description of Teilhard's scientific vision, we now want to ask how it is that he inserts the Christian phenomenon into this model. We speak of the Christian phenomenon since Christianity is in fact an historical reality, a piece of cosmic history enacted on planet earth. In the first place there is the reality of Jesus as a fact of history. Around this historical reality, a community of believers has grown through the years. And this religious community believes that in Jesus there has been a unique union of creation in its human form with the divine Word. This is the core content of the Christian dogma about Christ. It is in terms of this historical faith-tradition that Teilhard attempts to discern the proper name for the Omega point of the process which he has described from a scientific perspective. It is through his attempt to allow science and faith to intersect that he comes to speak of the goal of the cosmic process as Christ-Omega. And from this conjunction, he can see that the entire cosmic process is directed to that sort of fulfillment that is realized in the history of Jesus, the Christ. The all-pervasive movement of union is now seen to be evoked by the creative call of divine love that undergirds the entire history of the cosmos.

The Gospel command to love, then, is not merely a moral principle. It is the ontological principle of the development of creation. This power of love is dimly visible in the lower forms of evolution. But it can be seen there already as analogous with that power when it is adorned with personal qualities in humanity and is expressed in a single law: "Love one another." There is no other way into the future leading to the fullness of a creation that is invited to share in the life of the triune God. This is the answer God expects to the divine creative call of love.

Hence, the process of cosmic development can be seen as the shaping of a community of intelligent-loving beings centered in a community around Christ. In this sense Christ is essential for the final intelligibility of the process. But, writes Teilhard: "The mystical Christ has not yet attained to His full growth; and therefore the same is true of the cosmic Christ. . . . Christ is the end-point of the evolution, even the natural evolution, of all beings, and therefore evolution is holy."[12] And since the fruit of the process is finally the total Christ—Christ and the transformed cosmos with him— the entire process of cosmogenesis can finally be named Christogenesis.

In his *Commentary on Ecclesiastes* Bonaventure had written: "Each creature is a divine word because it says 'God.'"[13] In a similar way Teilhard sees the entire cosmos as a revelation of God. In the third part of *The Divine Milieu* he speaks of God's presence in the following words:

> God is revealed everywhere, beneath our groping efforts, as a *universal milieu,* only because God is *the ultimate point* upon which all realities converge. Each element of the world, whatever it may be, only subsists here and now in the manner of a cone whose lines meet in God, who draws them together. . . . It is precisely because God is infinitely profound and punctiform that God is infinitely near, and dispersed everywhere. It is precisely because God is the center that God fills the whole sphere.[14]

As a consequence of the incarnation, writes Teilhard, the divine immensity has transformed itself for us into the omnipresence of christification. The essence of Christianity consists in asking, when all is said and done, what is the real link that binds all these entities together and confers on them a final power of gaining hold of us? "The Christian answer is: The Word Incarnate, our Lord Jesus Christ . . . All the good that I can do . . . is physically gathered in . . . into the reality of the consummated Christ."[15]

Eucharist is, for Teilhard, the preeminent symbol and concrete sign of the divine Word's self-emptying into matter. But the mystery of Christ's presence is involved not only in the bread and wine. Christ comes sacramentally to each of the faithful to bind them more closely to himself and to all other faithful in the growing unity of the world. The act of transubstantiation extends itself beyond the bread and wine to the cosmos, which the

[12] *Hymn of the Universe,* (New York: Harper & Row, 1965) 133.
[13] *Opera omnia,* (VI, 16).
[14] *Divine Milieu,* 91.
[15] *Op. cit.,* 100–1.

continuing incarnation transforms. In a primary sense the body of Christ is limited to the eucharistic species. But the full meaning of this is seen in terms of the assimilation to all that surrounds Him in a way that is mystical.

> As our humanity assimilates the material world, and as the Host assimilates our humanity, the eucharistic transformation goes beyond and completes the transubstantiation of the bread on the altar. Step by step it irresistibly invades the universe. It is the fire that sweeps over the hearth; the stroke that vibrates through the bronze. In a secondary and generalized sense, but in a true sense, the sacramental species are formed by the totality of the world, and the duration of the creation is the time needed for its consecration. *In Christo vivimus, movemur, et sumus.*[16]

The model of incarnation helps unite the two ideas: Christ in the Eucharist and Christ in the world. Teilhard will support this by an appeal to Paul's theology of Christ the Head, in relation to the members of his body.

From this christological, eucharistic vision, Teilhard looks eventually to the end of history. "When Christ appears in the clouds, He will simply be manifesting a metamorphosis that has been slowly accomplished under His influence in the heart of the mass of humankind."[17] Teilhard's view is of the synthesis (not fusion) of God and creation as an extension or completion of the synthesis that has already taken place in the incarnation. Thus, it involves not only humans, but the whole of the material universe.

We can relate this to the traditional view found, for example, in medieval theology that in the end, body and soul will be reunited; and material reality will be transformed in the transformation of humanity, and thus be brought into the final synthesis. All Christian theology struggles with the task of putting this into intelligible categories. But it seems to say that, finally, the material world will not be annihilated. Rather, it will be radically transformed. What is distinctive of Teilhard is his attempt to speak of this as the outcome of the entire sweep of cosmic history.

But if we think of cosmic endings from the perspective of the only end that Christian faith believes it to have, that end is the fully gratuitous gift of God's transforming self-communication in love. This Christians believe has been realized in an anticipatory way in the resurrection of Christ. The creature is structured with a view to this utterly gratuitous self-gift of God. It is in its deepest core capable of receiving this depth of divine presence and of being transformed by it. In the language of the early Christian Fathers, as we have seen above, it is *capax Dei*. This is not a question of the natural structure demanding or having a right to grace. If that were the

---

[16] *Op. cit.,* 104.
[17] *Op. cit.,* 107.

case, we could no longer call it grace. It is, rather, a question of the offer of grace requiring the structure that makes it possible for grace to be received.

If, with Scotus, we say that God's first-intended is Christ, it seems consistent to say in Teilhard's context that the process of cosmic development has no other end than that. If this is, indeed, the goal of the process, then the entire process can be named from that fruit; it is a process of Christogenesis. Creation is the seed; cosmic development is the mode of the unfolding of God's creation; Omega is the fruit of the process.

IV) *Cosmic Christology and Contemporary Reflection*

Much of contemporary physics and cosmology operates on the conviction that there is a unifying principle in the created order. Christians precisely as believers share this conviction, but they have their own particular way of giving an account of what this might mean. Here we are concerned with the doctrine of creation in which the whole of the created order is seen as an expression of the divine creativity in action and as expressing the Wisdom or Word of God which is seen to be an inherent dimension of the nature of the divine.[18]

This unifying Word, while not limited to Christian experience, is believed by Christians to be embodied most emphatically in the history and person of Jesus of Nazareth. The specifically Christian affirmation is the claim that God was able to express something crucial concerning the divine nature in the historical human being, Jesus of Nazareth. It is the one divine Word through whom God creates that Christians believe to have become enfleshed most fully in Jesus of Nazareth. But the history of Jesus is a piece of the history of this planet and its immediate context. It can be discussed at this level without making any exaggerated claims about the rest of the universe. For Christians, the history of Jesus provides the clues for insight into the way in which God deals with humanity and its history. How God might deal with other forms of intelligent life, if they in fact exist, need not be the same. This would have to do with the peculiarities of their history.

If, however, there is one divine Wisdom/Word involved throughout the whole of creation, and if, in fact, there is intelligent, conscious life elsewhere, theology would expect that there would be some analogical relation between their destiny with God and human destiny with God. In other words, we can think of God's purpose as embodied in Jesus and its meaning for human life in this corner of our galaxy of this vast universe without necessarily claiming that this is the sole reason for the whole of the cosmos.

[18] A. Peacocke, *Theology for a Scientific Age* (Minneapolis: Fortress Press, 1993) 300ff.

We can think of the successful outcome of the existence of other intelligent forms without making that dependent on the history of Jesus.

We might suggest something like the following. In our effort to speak of the *why* of God's creative action, we might reach to the language of Whitehead and speak of God's ideal aim. From a specifically Christian perspective the ideal aim of God can be stated in the following way: God creates so that a final, life-giving synthesis of God and creation might be realized. This can be seen as a way of stating the meaning of the Christ-symbol formulated at the Council of Chalcedon: Truly God; truly human; united in one and the same concrete being. It is what historic Christianity believes has happened in Jesus, whom it calls the Christ. Interestingly as we have seen, in the tradition of cosmic christology, the incarnation does not enter in as an after-thought on the part of God because of sin. The so-called motive of the incarnation lies in the primordial, creative intent of God. The synthesis of God and world is what God intends from the beginning.

To what extent the divine aim will, in fact, be realized in the rest of humanity remains unknown. It is, therefore, an object of hope, not an object of knowledge. Christians have their own reasons for their hope that, finally, history will have a positive outcome that encompasses both humanity and the cosmos. But they do not know to what extent that hope will be fulfilled. It is because of their faith in the meaning of the Christ mystery that Christians may hope for a rich harvest of history, but they cannot claim to know how history will in fact work out, since the outcome of history depends deeply on human freedom.

The tradition of cosmic christology suggests the importance of reflecting on the relation of humanity to the chemical process of the cosmos. In terms of that context, how is one to envision the process that gives rise to human consciousness with all that implies? At one level, this chemical process is one of increasing complexification, and it is at this level of chemistry that consciousness is rooted in the larger patterns of the cosmos. If, in fact, we see this as a unified, cosmic unfolding, does this mean that human consciousness is well understood as the consciousness of the cosmos in us at this particular place and time of its history? This should not be understood to exclude the possibility that the cosmos has brought forth intelligent life and consciousness elsewhere, even though as yet we humans have no evidence of it.

For the Christian, therefore, Christ is not an intrusion into a world which can get along very well without him. Viewed in terms of our corner of the cosmos and its history, Christ can be seen as bringing the cosmic process to a new level of depth. He is, in Rahner's terms, what the entire history of life on this planet is about. In Rahner's view, Christ is that point in cosmic history where God's aim to communicate the divine self as fully as possible to the world becomes irreversible. And from the perspective of creation, Christ is that point at which the cosmos has opened itself up completely to the self-communication of God.

Seen from this perspective, the very fatalistic vision of cosmic history which frequently appears in contemporary physics can begin to take on a more human, personal quality without moving back into the excessively anthropocentric view of our recent past. Are we nothing but a futile episode in the vastness of space and time? Or do we exist *for* something? Theological reflection would suggest that, interesting as the phenomenon of mathematics may be, the final word about the universe may not be a purely mathematical formula. Finally, the cosmos is not about pure intelligibility and predictability, but about the mystery of the creative freedom of divine love in which the theological tradition sees both the contingency and purposefulness of creation to be grounded.

This christological orientation leads to a richer sense of how deeply our humanity is rooted in the chemistry of the universe. We exist in a situation of profound interrelation and interdependence with all cosmic reality. The God who we believe to be the creator brings the divine aim to fruition in and through the chemical processes of the cosmos. This awareness can lead to a deeper ethical sense of human responsibility for humanity's freely chosen ways of relating to the cosmos.

When we view the cosmos through the lense of modern science, we see an awe-inspiring cosmos which remains very ambiguous in terms of its possible meaning. When we view the same cosmos through the lense of Christian faith, we begin to discover a deeper sense of meaning and a richer sense of our place in this remarkable, unfolding, incomplete cosmos. We come gradually to a more hope-filled sense of our relation to the cosmic context of our existence.

9

Creation and the Future

I) *Scientific Visions of the Future*

Scientific cosmology opens to us a vision of a universe that is unfinished and open to a future. It is in the process of becoming over unimaginable reaches of time and space. Cosmologists have attempted to project backward to the beginning of this process. This leads to the idea of the Big Bang. But the thought of cosmologists does not stop there. The attempt is made also to project a possible future to the cosmic process. This is reflected in science in a number of different ways. Three major possibilities stand out. One is that the universe will continue to expand indefinitely. As this happens, the energy level will be lowered until it arrives at a temperature of absolute zero. This would be the so-called open model of the cosmos.

Another possibility is the closed model. It moves from the idea that at some point the expansion will stop and a movement of contraction will set in. The expansion that began with the Big Bang will end with a Big Crunch as everything collapses back into a cosmic melting pot with no extension in space but with what scientists speak of as infinite temperatures.

And a third view is the possibility of an ongoing series of recurring cycles of expansion and contraction. Whichever way one chooses to move in this area, the cosmic future that is envisioned is billions of years away. Long before any of that comes to pass—which will probably not be for another hundred billion years—we have a much more proximate future to look forward to, and that is the end of any form of life on planet earth when the sun becomes a red giant and makes the survival of life here impossible. This is projected in a mere five billion years.

From the perspective of the sciences, then, the question of the cosmic future is an area in which there is nothing close to a final answer. All scientific projections are highly speculative and hypothetical. But from a purely scientific viewpoint, for many scientists, the prospect is bleak. It is this background that has lead to the nihilistic statements found in many scientific writings. Bertrand Russell could write:

> . . . all the labors of all the ages, all the devotion, all the inspiration, all the noonday brightness of human genius, are destined to extinction in the vast death of the solar system, and . . . the whole temple of Man's (sic) achievement must inevitably be buried beneath the debris of a universe in ruins . . .[1]

Though this was written in 1903, the tone of it can be found in much of the scientific literature of the present. At the other end of the scientific spectrum are authors such as Freeman Dyson and Frank Tipler who, for quite different reasons, come to the conclusion that the universe is of such a sort that intelligent life will continue to exist forever.[2] But regardless of which end of the spectrum we look at, we are dealing with speculations about the meaning and the future of chemical, material reality.

II) *Christian Theology and the Future*

With this in mind, it is interesting to recall that the Christian religious tradition has long been convinced of the religious significance of material reality. In its creation theology, even in its classical form, it had seen creatures to be laden with potential for growth and development. Even more is that the case today when we think of the developing cosmos, and the development of life forms within it. For theology this raises the question of the nature of matter and the ultimate future of material reality.

We might think of the images of the book of Genesis that present human beings as responsible agents of God's creative care within creation. Such images suggest human responsibility for the future of the cosmos. And when we relate that to the vision of an evolutionary cosmos in which humanity has the power to set the future direction of the evolutionary process, the implications of this become more obvious. In its document on the mystery of the church, Vatican Council II speaks of the eschatological dimension of

---

[1] Bertrand Russell, "A Free Man's Worship," in *Mysticism and Logic, and other Essays* (London: Allen & Unwin, 1963) 41.

[2] Cfr. Freeman Dyson, "Time without End: Physics and Biology in an Open Universe," in *Reviews of Modern Physics* 51 (1977) 447; J. Barrow & F. Tipler, *The Anthropic Cosmological Principle* (New York: Oxford University Press, 1988); F. Tipler, *The Physics of Immortality* (New York: Doubleday, 1994).

Christian faith in the following way: "Then humanity and the entire world which is so intimately related to humanity will achieve its end through humanity and will be perfectly restored in Christ."[3]

Theology thinks of this future when it speaks of God's aim in creating. But to speak of a divine aim is not to say that the aim will be realized in its ideal form. God has created a world in which the realization of the divine aim depends on the interactions among creatures, particularly at the level of human creatures where we are dealing with freely chosen values and actions. As a God of love, God has created a world that is not ruled by force or coercion. The creative love of God can well be thought of as a power that "lets things be"; a power that calls creatures to realize the potential that lies within them. Process theology tends to think of God as the source of all possibilities; a God who does not push creatures out from a past, but who calls creatures from the future. Given the contemporary understanding of a developing cosmos, and developing species within it, and given the dynamic of development that seems to involve an interplay between chance and necessity, it might be more helpful to think of God not as the eternal Planner who has written a finished script for cosmic history which must be carried out, but rather to think of God as the Infinite Source of new possibilities. The cosmos is open to a real future, and that future finally is the fruit of cosmic and human history responding to the possibilities offered by God.[4]

As we have seen above in discussing the tradition of cosmic christology, there is a sense in which the figure of Christ belongs to the architecture of the cosmos. It is the dogma of Chalcedon that has formulated the decisive insight concerning the coming together of God and creation in the figure of the incarnate Word. It is in the Christian affirmation of the resurrection of Christ that the Christian tradition comes to its convictions concerning the future of God's creation. The Pauline use of the metaphor of the seed that must be planted is helpful in evoking this sense of future fulfillment:

> But someone will say, "How are the dead raised? With what kind of body will they come back?" You fool. What you sow is not brought to life unless it dies. And what you sow is not the body that is to be but a bare kernel of wheat, perhaps, or of some other kind; but God gives it a body as he chooses, and to each of the seeds its own body. . . . So is the resurrection of the dead. It is sown corruptible; it is raised incorruptible. It is sown dishonorable; it is raised glorious. It is sown weak; it is raised powerful. It is sown a natural body; it is raised a spiritual body (1 Cor 15:35-44).

[3] *Lumen gentium* #48. The conciliar text refers to the following biblical sources: Eph 1:10; Col 1:20; and 2 Pet 3:10-13.

[4] Cfr. Haught, *God after Darwin*, for an extended and systematic discussion of this perspective.

A text of St. John points in a similar direction: "Beloved, we are God's children now. What we shall be has not yet been revealed. We do know that when it is revealed, we shall be like him, for we shall see him as he is" (1 John 3:2).

The relation between creation, incarnation, and resurrection may be helpful, then, in stimulating reflections on the issue of the future from a theological perspective. The sciences today help us to see how deeply humanity is embedded in the chemistry of the universe. Theologically, both the chemical universe and humanity have a meaning which is to be read from the mystery of Christ. His person and destiny point to the kind of future which humanity may hope for, and to the life style that is appropriate when we view ourselves in the light of that future.

As we have seen in discussing the question of origins, the theological concept of creation is not a question about some first moment of time as the point of origin. It is first and foremost the idea of a non-temporal mystery of absolute origin in God. In a similar way the question of the ultimate future is not a question of theology extending the line of cosmic time to a specific future point, however distant that may be. Rather, the Christian hope in the future is the deepest extension of the biblical trust in the fidelity of God who creates for a purpose, and who will not desert the world that is God's own creation. The future to which God calls the world is not an indefinite extension of the space-time context of the present world. It is rather the question of the final transforming relation between the created world and God that moves creation to a new level of being. This final state is understood to involve the most perfect exchange of love between God and creation, through which creation is brought to its transforming fulfillment.

How might this religious, christological vision relate to the open-ended sense of cosmic evolution, and to the question of the meaning of conscious life which emerges out of the process of cosmic chemistry? Surely a cosmic christology would allow us to see the open-endedness of the cosmos not so much as a threat of ultimate extinction, but as a sacramental sign of the divine promise of a yet fuller, richer existence than that which we now know but which can come to be only through human and cosmic history. But the Christian vision of the future is not simply a question of the immanent, worldly development of creaturely potential through creaturely effort. This immanent, cosmic development may be seen as a crucial condition for that future. But the future is finally the ultimate, transforming self-gift of God to creation which brings the whole of created reality to its final fruition. Christian eschatology is not a question of the ultimate extension of evolution, nor is it an ideology of inevitable historical progress. It is, above all, a question of radical transformation through the loving, creative power of the divine. Such a vision can help relieve the sense of cosmic terror which threatens those who contemplate the vast reaches of space and time which constitute the cosmic context of human existence as we know it today.

The sort of conversation between theology and the sciences that we have been concerned with throughout this book will mean that theology may have to engage in significant redefinition and reformulation of many areas of its concern. Specifically, our understanding of salvation and the relation of salvation to the destiny of the cosmos is in serious need of reformulation. We need to relocate the meaning of salvation within the context of creation-theology. Christ's destiny anticipates in one human being the universal aim of God in creating. Language about salvation, then, is primarily about the fullness of life and experience that God intends in creating. It is, in Whitehead's terms, the "ideal aim" of God, the Creator. Language about redemption, on the other hand, with its negative overtones is principally about overcoming the obstacles to that fullness.

The tradition had long ago said that grace does not destroy nature. On the contrary, grace presupposes nature and brings it to perfection. While this principle applied first of all to human nature, it can well be extended to take in human nature's relation to the broader cosmic context within which humanity is situated. Both grace and eschatological fulfillment, as moments in the theological understanding of salvation, need to be seen as moments in the process by which God is bringing the cosmos to completion through history.

As we have seen above, to speak of the future theologically raises the question of eschatology. The relation between the doctrine of creation and that of eschatology was already pointed out in our discussion of the Scriptures. Creation is to be thought of in relation to the new creation. The theme of the new creation appears strongly in the literature of the prophets and in the inter-testamental apocalyptic literature. In the Christian Scriptures the central metaphor of the future is that of the resurrection. In the destiny of Jesus Christ is seen the anticipation of the destiny of creation. Thus, the world that has been decisively touched by the power of divine love in the mystery of Christ now awaits its final fulfillment.

But this period of waiting is not to be seen as a period of inactivity. If the personal history of Jesus was the presupposition for the final outcome of that history even though the final outcome of his life is the preeminent gift of God, so the history of the human race may be seen as the presupposition for the final outcome, even though in the deepest sense, the final outcome is a gift of God. We might say that the new creation is not a creation from nothing, but a new creation from out of the old creation. In this sense the hope for the future should not turn our minds and hearts away from this world of God's creation, but it should inspire us to take the world and our relation to it very seriously; for human history and cosmic history is the material from which God will create the new order.

Thus it is appropriate that, in contemporary theology, the preaching of the Gospel frequently moves into the area of social criticism and a call to action in the social realm for the sake of transforming the world already now. The reflections of Vatican II in *Gaudium et spes* speak of the inner renewal of the human spirit through the Spirit of the risen Christ.[5] The text goes on to underline the mystery of the incarnation through which Christians discover the most profound sense in which Christians come to claim that God is love (1 John 4:8). "At the same time He (= Christ) taught us that the new command of love was the basic law of human perfection and hence of the world's transformation."[6] Thus, the Council urges us to work for the renewal of human society on a broad scale. Speaking of the new earth and the new heaven, the Council writes:

> While charity and its fruits endure, all of creation which God has made for the sake of humanity will be unchained from the bondage of vanity. Therefore, while we are warned that it profits us nothing to gain the whole world and lose ourselves, the expectation of a new earth must not weaken but rather must stimulate our concern for cultivating this one. For here grows the body of a new human family, a body which, even now, is able to give some foreshadowing of the new age.[7]

Having offered this word of encouragement for Christians to be involved in the transformation of the world of human society, the Council makes it clear that human and social progress should not be identified with the Kingdom of God: "Earthly progress must be carefully distinguished from the growth of Christ's Kingdom. Nevertheless, to the extent that the former can contribute to the better ordering of human society, it is of vital concern to the kingdom of God."[8]

The Christian vision of reality lives from the conviction that eventually the world will be brought to completion. Already at the prehuman level, the cosmic process has been bringing about transformation to ever new forms, eventually coming to intelligent life. Now, in humanity, nature is capable of consciously choosing what sort of transformation will be involved in shaping our future. The Christian vision, with its eye on Christ, looks to a transformation through the power of self-sacrificing love. In the power of such love the network of relations in which humanity finds itself will be brought to a new level of depth, and the cosmos together with humanity

[5] *Gaudium et spes*, n. 22–24.
[6] *Op. cit.*, n. 38.
[7] *Op. cit.*, n. 39.
[8] *Ibid.*

and through humanity's response to God will be opened to the final fulfilling, transforming self-gift of God.

Our theology of creation begins with the conviction that our very being is a pure gift from a loving, creative God. As we experience our existence within history, it is a gift laden with potential to develop into ever deeper, richer realizations. Precisely what its definitive form will be like we cannot claim to know. But the Christian belief in the incarnation and resurrection of Jesus Christ challenges us to remain open to the mystery that the created universe is and can yet become. Image and metaphor is the primary language used to elicit a sense of that future, but such language is not descriptive of the reality that awaits us.

Christian faith, then, is a hope-filled openness to the future. At one level, it is receptive. We first receive the gift of being without having been consulted. As we receive the gift of being in our birth, so we are called to receive the consummation of that gift in a future that transcends death. But the being which we receive, and the potential with which it is laden, awaken us to an active response. What we make of ourselves and of our world is crucial for the final, transforming self-gift of God by which God brings creation to its completion.

Bibliography

Science and Theology

Barbour, Ian, *Religion in an Age of Science* (San Francisco: HarperCollins, 1990).

Blackwell, Richard J., *Galileo, Bellarmine, and the Bible* (Notre Dame, Ind.: University of Notre Dame Press, 1991).

Gould, Stephen Jay, *Rocks of Ages: Science and Religion in the Fullness of Life* (New York: Ballantine, 1999).

Haught, John, *Science and Religion: From Conflict to Conversation* (Mahwah, N.J.: Paulist Press, 1995).

Langford, Jerome J., *Galileo, Science, and the Church* (South Bend, Ind.: St. Augustine's Press, 1998).

Peacocke, Arthur, *Theology for a Scientific Age: Being and Becoming—Natural, Divine, and Human* (Minneapolis: Fortress Press, 1993).

Polkinghorne, John, *Science and Theology: An Introduction* (Minneapolis: Fortress Press, 1998).

Scripture

Anderson, Bernard, *From Creation to New Creation: Old Testament Perspectives* (Minneapolis: Fortress Press, 1994).

Clifford, Richard, and John Collins, eds. *Creation in the Biblical Traditions* (Catholic Biblical Monograph Series 24, Catholic Biblical Association of America, Washington, D.C., 1992).

Collins, Raymond, *Letters That Paul Did Not Write: The Epistle to the Hebrews and the Pauline Pseudoepigrapha* (Wilmington, Del.: M. Glazier, 1988).

Fitzmyer, Joseph, *Paul and His Theology: A Brief Sketch,* 2 ed. (Englewood Cliffs, N.J.: Prentice Hall, 1989).

Karris, Robert, *The Pastoral Epistles* (Wilmington, Del.: M. Glazier, 1979).

Lohfink, Norbert, *Theology of the Pentateuch: Themes of the Priestly Narrative and Deuteronomy,* tr. L. Maloney (Minneapolis: Fortress Press, 1994).

Westermann, Claus, *Genesis 1-11: A Commentary* (Minneapolis: Augsburg, 1984).

Creation from Nothing

Haught, John, *God after Darwin: A Theology of Evolution* (Boulder, Colo.: Westview Press, 2000).

May, Gerhard, *Creatio ex nihilo: The Doctrine of 'Creation out of Nothing' in Early Christian Thought,* tr. A. S. Worrall (Edinburgh: Edinburgh, 1994).

Moltmann, Jürgen, *God and Creation: A New Theology of Creation and the Spirit of God* (Minneapolis: Fortress Press, 1993).

Worthing, Mark William, *God, Creation, and Contemporary Physics* (Minneapolis: Fortress Press, 1996).

The Problem of Evolution

Barrow, J., F. Tipler, *The Anthropic Cosmological Principle* (Oxford, N.Y.: Oxford University Press, 1988).

Greene, John C., *Debating Darwin: Adventures of a Scholar* (Claremont, Calif.: ReginaBooks, 1999).

Hefner, Philip J., *The Human Factor: Evolution, Culture, and Religion* (Minneapolis: Fortress Press, 1993).

Peters, T., ed., *Science and Theology: The New Consonance* (Boulder, Colo.: Westview Press, 1998).

Ratzinger, Cardinal Joseph, *"In the Beginning . . ." A Catholic Understanding of the Story of Creation and the Fall,* tr. B. Ramsey (Huntington, Ind.: Our Sunday Visitor, 1990).

Sin and Evil

Gilkey, Langdon, "The God of Nature," in: *Chaos and Complexity: Scientific Perspectives on Divine Action,* ed. R. Russell, N. Murphy, A. Peacocke (Vatican City and Berkeley, Calif.: 1995) 211–20.

Korsmeyer, Jerry D., *Evolution and Eden: Balancing Original Sin and Contemporary Science* (Mahwah, N.J.: Paulist Press, 1998).

Rolston III, Holmes, "Does Nature Need to be Redeemed?" in *Zygon* 29 (1994) 2:205ff.

Cosmic Christology

Edwards, Denis, *Jesus and the Cosmos* (Mahwah, N.J.: Paulist Press, 1991).

Edwards, Denis, *Jesus and the Wisdom of God: An Ecological Theology* (Maryknoll, N.Y.: Orbis Press, 1995).

Hayes, Zachary, *What Manner of Man? Sermons on Christ by St. Bonaventure* (Chicago: Franciscan Herald Press, 1974).

King, Ursula, *The Spirit of One Earth: Reflections on Teilhard de Chardin and Global Spirituality* (New York: Paragon House, 1989).

McElrath, Damian, ed. *Franciscan Christology* (St. Bonaventure, N.Y.: Franciscan Institute Publications, 1980).

Peacocke, Arthur, *Theology for a Scientific Age* (Minneapolis: Fortress Press, 1993).

Polkinghorne, John, *The Faith of a Physicist* (Princeton, N.J.: Princeton University Press, 1994).

Schmitz-Moormann, Karl, *Theology of Creation in an Evolutionary World,* with J. F. Salmon (Cleveland: Pilgrim Press, 1997).

Index of Names and Topics